L.O.V.E. works!

photojournalism by the Leave Out ViolencE teens

Edited by Brenda Zosky Proulx

Published in 1998 by Stoddart Publishing Co. Limited
34 Lesmill Road, Toronto, Canada M3B 2T6
180 Varick Street, 9th Floor, New York, New York 10014

Distributed in Canada by:
General Distribution Services Ltd.
325 Humber College Blvd.,Toronto, Ontario M9W 7C3
Tel. (416) 213-1919 Fax (416) 213-1917
Email customer.service@ccmailgw.genpub.com

Distributed in the United States by:
General Distribution Services Inc.
85 River Rock Drive, Suite 202, Buffalo, New York 14207
Toll-free Tel. 1-800-805-1083 Toll-free Fax 1-800-481-6207
Email gdsinc@genpub.com

02 01 00 99 98 1 2 3 4 5

Canadian Cataloguing in Publication Data

Main entry under title:
L.O.V.E. works: photojounalism by the Leave Out ViolencE kids

ISBN 0-7737-6008-3

1. Violence – Prevention – Pictorial works .
2. Violence – Prevention – Literary collections.
3. Juvenile delinquency – Prevention – Pictorial works.
4. Juvenile delinquency – Prevention – Literary collections.
I. Zosky Proulx, Brenda. II. Leave Out ViolencE (Association).
HV9069.L68 1998 364.4'0222 C98-931458-8

Photo opposite Contents page:
"Ignorance breeds violence," by Melissa Colley.

Design: Andrew Smith
Page Composition: Joseph Gisini/Andrew Smith Graphics Inc.
Printed and bound in Canada

This work is dedicated to the memory of Daniel E. Rudberg,
who lost his life in pursuit of justice at the age of 38 on September 30, 1972.
Because of the nature of his death and the triumph of positive choice,
the Leave Out ViolencE organization was founded in 1993.

L.O.V.E. Works! is also dedicated to the youth of this world
whose lives are affected by violence on a daily basis. More often than not
they are the victims of social injustice. Their voices must be heard.

*"Mourn not the dead, but rather mourn the apathetic throng,
the cowed and the meek who see the world's great anguish and its wrong
and dare not speak."*

— INSCRIPTION ON DANIEL RUDBERG'S TOMBSTONE

Leave Out ViolencE is an organization that helps young people reject violence.
We win many and, sadly, we lose some, but we keep on trying
because we know that whatever change we effect is better than no change at all.

The future of our youth is everyone's responsibility.

MATHQUEST 8

Contents

Special Thanks to the following
GOLD SUPPORTERS
who believe "The future of our youth is everyone's responsibility"

Nani & Austin Beutel
The Edward Bronfman Family Foundation
The Samuel & Saidye Bronfman Family Foundation
The Chawkers Foundation
CIBC Wood Gundy Children's Miracle Foundation
CORLAB/CORMONT
Janette & Michael Diamond
e3m Investments Inc.
Ehmjaykay
The John Baker Fellowes Family Foundation
First Marathon Securities
Nancy & Marc Gold
Harry L. Hopmeyer
IMI International
Gustav Levinschi Foundation
Pearl & Saul Lighter
McDonald's Restaurants of Canada Limited
Bank of Montreal
Dora & Avi Morrow
Nisker Associates Inc.
Onex Corporation
Royal Bank of Canada Charitable Foundation
Twinkle Rudberg
ScotiaMcLeod
Jim Stein
TD Bank Financial Group
The Trillium Foundation
Lois & Stanley Tucker
United Way of Greater Toronto
Velan Inc.
Whitecastle Investments Limited
Zeller Family Foundation
Anonymous

All Gold Supporters have given $5000 or more for L.O.V.E.'s 1998 Youth Violence Prevention Programming

Preface

By Brenda Zosky Proulx

It is said that violent acts can be traced back to that hollow place inside the human spirit where self-esteem was meant to be.

How is it, then, that this essential element of well-being has been stolen from the core of our disenchanted youth? Where has it gone? And how can we get it back?

There are some answers here, in this compelling book and within the hearts of the courageous L.O.V.E. youths who are its sole authors and photographers. Their raw words and photos help us to understand why we face a crisis of youth violence in this society and what we need to do to repair the damage.

On one level, many of them are exactly the kinds of kids who strike fear into the hearts of the mainstream. Some have been deeply involved with drugs or incarcerated for having stolen, stabbed, or beaten. A number have been the victims of violence themselves, at home or on the street, and a few have victimized other children. Several have been both perpetrators and victims. Finally, some have been touched by violence by living on its fringes, or by losing someone they love to it.

No matter what their past, they joined the L.O.V.E. team because they realized that violence doesn't solve anything. They made a commitment to try to reverse the skyrocketing incidence of youth violence — first by turning their own lives around, and then by helping others to do the same. To this end, they embarked on a journey into youth culture today, beginning with their own realities, no matter how dark and troubled. Armed with a camera, a pen, and a note pad, they set out to look for explanations and for hope.

Although they were referred to us by teachers, community workers, police, and parole officers, their participation in the L.O.V.E. project is completely voluntary. They gathered after school in windowless college basements and photo labs to discuss, to write, and to develop their film. Their reporting focused on three themes: What are the causes of youth violence? What is its impact on all of our lives? How can we eliminate it?

Their product — this jarring, poignant book — is a wakeup call!

As families and communities continue to disintegrate; as youth face the despair of a shrinking job market; as working in the drug trade presents an ever-attractive alternative; as our education system flounders under crushing pressures;

as teens from various cultural groups find themselves living nose to nose without the tools to negotiate differences with compassion and tolerance; and as the media pound them with relentless images of violence, what can we expect?

This book is a wakeup call that could *only* have come from the kids who are living the crisis. And what is their message? They are telling us that the social systems which underlie the causes of youth violence have to change. Families need more support. Schools too. The business community must open its heart and give our youth part-time jobs where they can learn skills and hope. We must work harder to break down the fearful barriers between cultural groups which breed aggression, and the media must at last reject violence as a marketing strategy to feed its bottom line. This is what these kids are telling us and we must listen, because, so far, the so-called "experts" have not come up with solutions to the alarming increase in youth violence.

In my mind, the L.O.V.E. kids are our unsung heroes, calling out to us while often in the throes of painful life-and-death struggles themselves. They have earned my respect because of their willingness to confront their demons and move on. No matter what they've done or what has been done to them, they are not willing to accept a violence-ridden society. They are looking for hope. The hope is them.

The L.O.V.E. photojournalism project that produced this book came out of a collaboration between the late and much-missed Clifton Ruggles, a gifted artist and passionate teacher, Stan Chase, a devoted educator and photography technician, and me, a writer and journalism professor. Clifton inspired and enriched us. Stan and I are the lucky ones who work with the kids at Dawson College in Montreal with the help of a variety of committed assistants, including journalists Diana Ballon and Buffy Childerhose, and photographers David Janes and Maureen Labreche. We then took it to Toronto where Dana Zosky, L.O.V.E.'s executive director in Ontario, journalism professor Shelley Robertson, journalist Jill Borra, photography instructor and photographer Philip Taylor, and photographer Cathy Bidini now run a second program at Ryerson Polytechnic University.

The photographs and writings in this book form part of a travelling exhibit which L.O.V.E. teenagers take into schools, community organizations, and youth detention centres for use as mentoring tools.

Our goal is to give youth a chance to produce quality work that inspires other teenagers to turn their own lives around and builds a bridge of understanding between youth on the edge and the community that often fears them.

L.O.V.E. Story

By Twinkle Rudberg

On September 30, 1972, my life changed forever. That day my husband, Daniel Rudberg, was murdered by a 14-year-old boy. It was an event that changed the lives of those who loved Daniel, all of us who had never experienced the horror of murder. How could we suddenly have lost this vibrant, beautiful young man of 38, a father, a husband, a son, a brother, an engineer with a bright future ahead of him.

This story began with a young boy whose cries of loneliness and frustration had found no ear. A young boy who had been raised by television, who had been left to fend for himself, who had no family structure or community to draw upon. He turned to drugs. He joined a gang. He ran away from his home and turned to violence to feed his loneliness, imitating the acts he had witnessed so often on the TV screen that kept him company.

It was a Saturday night in Montreal. Daniel and I were on our way to dinner with four friends when we witnessed a barefoot boy jump out of the back seat of a car and mug an older woman. He ran off with her purse. Dan stopped our car, got out, and helped the victim up. He then pursued the 14-year-old into some bushes. The teen pulled a small knife that he later said he had "designated for some hero" and used it to murder Daniel.

I thought my life had ended.

Everyone in this story became a victim of violence that day. It took me many years and much soul searching to recognize that the teen was a victim as well — a victim of circumstance, a victim of our society, a prisoner of what had been dealt to him.

I asked myself how many of us, how many more of our youth must become victims before we all wake up and try to change what never should have happened to our children. I had been asleep and suddenly my eyes opened wide and I knew that I had a choice to make. Do I live the rest of my life as a victim? Do I wait to hear of more families suffering the pain that I have experienced, or do I take the lessons learned and use them to try and stop the epidemic of violence in our youth?

I have come to believe that events happen for a reason. Each of us has a responsibility to act on the lessons that are put in our path so as to make sense of them.

It was with this in mind that I formed a group of committed members of our communities to start the Leave Out ViolencE project. We all wanted to work for change. We had watched youth violence proliferate to an alarming degree, and we recognized that if we didn't deal with the root cause of this problem there would be many more victims. We created projects that grew and began to have an amazing effect for the good. We became a force for change.

I know that I have made the right choice for my life when I visit classrooms with our teen outreach teams and hear the testimonies of violence, fear, and abuse from 9-year-old children through to high school; when I hear a young boy say that, yes, he has seen someone killed by a gun, "It was my Father and I was 8"; when I see the glazed eyes of young, powerful boys and girls who say that their only reference point is violence, that their future depends on how aggressive they can be to survive — in the schoolyard, in their homes, in their gangs; when a young man says to me that if it weren't for L.O.V.E. he would either be dead or in jail; when I look into a 16-year-old's eyes and see the desperation as he says, "Please help me get out of my gang or I will be dead by 20"; when kids come up to us and say please help us, we are frightened. When I hear all this, I know I have made the right choice for my life's work.

These young people do not want violence in their lives . . . they want to be heard, they want to live in peace. These teens hate every moment of the trap that they are in. They want the voice that we are giving them.

I believe in these young people. I recognize in them a wealth of talent, heart, and soul. They are our most valuable asset and we must not ignore them. Their voice and their anger, properly channelled, is what will make a difference to our world.

Yes, I am often sad that I was denied the privilege of having a husband to be my partner, and of living with my children in a full family unit. But we have all survived with strength.

I feel that I have been truly blessed to be a part of the work that L.O.V.E. is doing, to have become a community with these wonderful teens. I feel honoured to have had the privilege of working with people of great talent and huge hearts. I feel encouraged by the open response of some individuals, foundations, and corporations when I approach them for funding. I respect their generosity of spirit and their sense of responsibility to our youth. I feel encouraged by the response of our governments, who are beginning to support initiatives for prevention instead of punishment.

I know that the Leave Out ViolencE kids' movement will grow with strength and volume into the next millennium. I pray that their words and voices will help to make the 21st century a time of peace, in a world with less violence and more LOVE. We have all been blessed by angels.

welcome to L.O.V.E.

I remember a time when I could run around and do whatever I wanted without worrying that anything could harm me. But then again, I was only a child. Now, I'm 17, but in my short life span I have seen gang fights, drug running, bootlegging, people with no homes. I remember going to court and seeing more than half of my friends at the court house. Everyone I talked to was getting charged with something or other, from shoplifting to attempted murder . . .

Since I was a kid I have been part of this disgusting scene. I have gotten into fights over nothing more than a few words of nonsense. I have had my head bashed between doors and arms beaten purple and blue with my own school binder. I have seen my parents fight to the point that plates of food fly past my head and through the window into the yard where my brothers play.

I have seen and heard pretty much all that a person of 17 can experience in the field of violence. I have beat and I have been beaten, and I had become numb. I'm not saying I'm a mean person, it's just that you have to act a certain way on the street.

The Leave Out ViolencE program opened my mind and showed me the problems with violence in today's society. It has opened doors for me as well. I can honestly say that without this program I do not know where I would be today.

Charles Wagge, 17*

** Indicates age of writer when piece was written*

Love will someday rule the world.

PHOTO BY SABRINA SMITH / CAPTION BY SAIMA BAIG

I'm a 17-year-old black girl living on the streets on Montreal, Quebec, Canada.

Montreal? Most people will think: "Oh, what is she complaining about? It's not like any of the inner city streets in the States!" But au contraire! I have seen and experienced things that would normally make someone go crazy.

Down in my old area I've seen men beat women, not only in my household, but on the streets. Syringes, blood on the streets, cops attacking friends of mine.

People dying away from my heart.

They're memories still alive and true. A little girl at the age of 9, crying herself to sleep, asking herself: "Why do people do this to each other?" "How come it doesn't stop?" They're memories of my mind, and still to this day I don't have the answer to those questions.

So when I heard a year ago about this group (L.O.V.E.), I knew that finally I can make a difference to the world, to my community, and to my inner soul.

This group has finally helped me to understand that maybe violence isn't something that the world plans on doing. Maybe it comes from something they feel inside, like anger, despair, pain, and evil.

Melissa Colley, 17

I've seen people dying . . . dying away from my heart.

PHOTO BY EMMIE SHEAFE / CAPTION BY MELISSA COLLEY

I joined L.O.V.E. because it was a chance to express a view on violence. But I always felt that I was writing from a certain distance.

Until a good friend turned to violence. Until another friend lost a friend to violence. Until I felt fear when a dangerous criminal was hiding in my apartment building.

I hope this book helps adults see through our eyes. I hope this book will help youths understand and realize that they can do something about violence. After all, just look at what we did.

Junie Desil, 18

I was a little boy when I realized that violence existed . . .

That it had been with us from the beginning.

It has always brought nothing but tears, death, and evil among us.

Today I'm a teenager and tomorrow is soon.

But I'm sick of it.

Tired of being scared.

Tired of walking alone with my thoughts.

I want it to leave us alone forever.

That's why I'm in L.O.V.E.

Nicholas Ramirez, 17

I don't know why I'm in this project.
I don't know why I even deserve to live.
But I guess if I wasn't here I'd
Be lying in some hole, fried out of my mind.
I'm starting to find the pieces, the missing pieces
To the puzzle.
I hope the puzzle is soon finished.

Jesse Sicinski, 14

I see violence on a daily basis, but I know that there are many people who don't have to face it. They don't have to be afraid of gangs, or of a city out of control. For me, unfortunately, that isn't real life. I have to face violence almost every day, either in the streets or in the alleyways or just places I hang out. I know what gangs are. I know the real world. I experienced drugs, I have seen drivebys . . . This violence has to be stopped, so I've taken a stand. I joined the Leave Out ViolencE program and I'm trying to make a difference in my community. We all have to speak up and say you are never safe in a gang, but you are safe once you decide to change and become a good person.

Justin Fullerton, 15

Brace Yourself

One way . . . one try.

PHOTO AND CAPTION BY NICHOLAS RAMIREZ

PHOTO BY HEATHER WRIGHT

Pool of Blood

I remember playing basketball on the neighborhood court and hearing a boy run down the hill yelling, "Please no," and the sound of a gun going off and his body rolling down the rest of the hill and him lying in a pool of blood.

When the gun went off I began to look frantically for my little brother. I was running and yelling out my brother's name. But it wasn't easy finding him. I was pushed and shoved but I didn't stop looking.

When I finally found him, I told him to follow me but all he did was stand there. "What's wrong?" I asked. He responded, "I can't move." By now everyone is running and screaming, I wanted to get out of there so I grabbed my brother's hand and told him nothing was going to happen to him. I wouldn't let it, and with that we ran for home.

When we were running, tons of tears were running down my face. My stomach felt like someone was trying to pull it out.

Our mother was running towards us because she heard what happened. When she saw us, she ran even faster and gave us each big hugs and kisses for at least two minutes. The weird thing about this whole mess is that the whole time I kept thinking, I don't want my brother to see this.

Pool of Blood

Melissa Samuel, 15

Violence in Entertainment

Violence in entertainment becomes violence in our environment. When I come out of a violent movie, I feel like going back to my bad self, because when you see it you say "that's the way life is" and then give up.

I know because I have been in that situation so many times. Right now I am working hard, but I don't have it easy . . . like my whole life . . . so when I see a violent movie it brings me back, and I say "Why bother trying?"

Eve Hill, 17

Violence in Entertainment

Poverty

Broken glass littering the ground. Decaying buildings with broken window panes. Once symbols of looking out towards the future, now symbols of dashed hopes and dreams. The air reeks of rotten garbage, of despair, of a never-ending cycle of poverty.

Poverty, an unfortunate social condition our society is plagued with and unfortunately it affects youth the most. Poverty plays a major role in violence among youths. Teens that are poor tend to be dropouts, or at risk of dropping out. They tend to live in a single-parent family unit or in a family where the situation is unbearable. They tend to live in terrible conditions. For the teen there is no hope. It is a never ending cycle, and in desperation or because it is the only way, they turn to a life of crime. Stealing something or selling drugs to make money, etc.

Poverty

Junie Desil, 17

As a humanity, we must fix things on the planet. PHOTO BY JEREMY DUCHARME / CAPTION BY SEMIRA WEISS

Racism

Racism is like murder, a crime for putting
someone down for the colour of their skin, which
shouldn't be allowed. If you can't stop it,
Who can?

Racism is like having an elephant walk
all over you or a spell that in time will
destroy all.

Racism is like the pollution that no one
tries to stop. Standing on a fire or getting
your legs chopped off is how it feels.
If you can't stop it, who can?

Racism is like having a knife go through
your heart over and over again just to
get a laugh. But it really hurts.

Racism is like having a nightmare every day
of your life, and only the victims never
forget. If you can't stop it, who can?

Miranda Collins, 16

An Event

It was a grey day and my brothers and I were nervous as it was our first day. We were in the school yard when I was called "nigger."

I didn't know what it meant, but I knew it wasn't good. The guy looked threatening and I was scared. He said "nigger" and other things which I can't remember. The last time he said "nigger" he started pushing me around, and then we got into a fight. When the yard monitor pulled me off he sent me inside.

I asked my teacher what "nigger" meant. She wouldn't tell me. She said it was harmless and I was overreacting. I was mad.

Later I checked the word "nigger" in the dictionary. The funny thing was, a couple years later we met up and the first thing he said was "sorry." We were friends after that. He explained that his parents were ignorant. His mother's attitude towards visible minorities started to change. I'm not sure about his father though.

An Event

Junie Desil, 17

One violent act causes a chain of violent acts. PHOTO AND CAPTION BY PHILIPPE MARTINS

A Dim Light

Dim light alone in the darkness rattled by the screams of terror echoing from the emptiness that surrounds. The light so fragile in its glass case, so close to breaking but holds to the socket just to maintain the flow of electricity that sustains it. The room is made brighter and the image of a boy is seen as a shadow.

There he sits staring at the floor looking at the tears as they fall making a weak sound that goes unnoticed by all except him. Trying to understand and make sense of the madness all around and in his own mind with only himself to talk to. Contained in a room with white walls a place of thought, a sanctuary for the pain that overwhelms him. He looks to the toys on his bright yellow dresser and the poster on his door of a lion for reassurance and understanding.

A crashing sound of dishes shatters his nerves, cracking the glass case that contains the light of his soul and losing all hope he buries his head in his pillow, knowing that nothing will save him.

A Dim Light

My Brother

Sharing flesh and blood, thoughts and pain, but not knowing each other just the same
Wanting to help this younger me, can't walk through flames of agony.
Call as you do with the look in your eyes, damned if I don't and damned if I try.
Wish you could understand the guilt I feel, but the fear holds me just the same.
Crying at night, praying for peace.
The tears that fall a double reflection of both our faces.

My Brother

both pieces by Malcolm Nadeau, 18

The security of the park has been ruined. PHOTO AND CAPTION BY ALI MOSADEQ

You Lied

You told me you would never hurt me,
You said you'd never leave me.
You told me you would always love me.
You lied to me.

You said we were going to live on a farm.
You told me I could have lots of animals.
You said I could have my own room.
You lied to me again.

You told me I was a mistake.
You said I deserved to die.
You told me I was always bad.
You lied to me even more.

I know the truth.

You always hurt me.
You made it so that I was taken away.
You never did care about or love me.

We lived with your friends.
We had no animals.
We all had to share rooms.

I was the only one planned.
I don't deserve to die.
I was beaten for nothing.

You always lied to me.

You Lied

Miranda Collins, 16

Mother

When I ask you for help mother, why don't you help me?
When I shed a tear mother, why don't you ask if I'm all right?
When he strikes me mother, why do you leave me?
When you see me in pain mother, why don't you attempt to heal me?
When the agony is overwhelming, where are you mother?
When I scream for you, can you hear me mother?
When I disrespect you mother, can you understand me?
When I want to hit you with the kitchen chair mother,
ask yourself why.

Where have you been? Why are you so *blind*? Are you *immune* to compassion?
Where's the love, the laughter, the mother I used to know? My heart is empty.
You have no place in my world, you are no longer wanted in my life mother.

DO YOU UNDERSTAND ME MOTHER? WHEN I MOST NEED YOU, I CAN'T
FIND YOU, MOTHER.

When I ask for your help, I want it.
When I shed a tear, I want your attention.
When he hits me, I want you to see.
When I hurt, I want your healing.
When the agony is overwhelming, I want you to hold me.
When I scream, hear me.
When I hate you, I love you, yet when I love you I hate you.

I need you, mother.

Teria Delaportas, 18

Her Pain

Very young her life
was full of sadness,
tears that needed someone
to help dry them up.

At home she felt distrustful,
fearful and worthless.
Her attempts to gain approval
only made for more trauma and despair.

Her mother was cruel and brutal,
expecting perfection
from her little victim.
She was emotionally hurting, too,
but falsely believed taking drastic measures
would reveal her trauma.

Years passed and the abuse worsened —
screams and cries for help travelled through the walls,
scars left from heavy blows,
tears fell harder,
anger and resentment slowly added
to her victim's eyes.

Her victim grew up.
Not one trace of self-esteem left,
she treats herself the way
her mom treated her.

If only someone would show her
how wonderful and gracious she is,
she would grow into the person
her mother didn't want to see.
She would surely blossom.

Anne-Marie Raffoul, 15

They say it's a progressive society but . . . PHOTO AND CAPTION BY NICHOLAS RAMIREZ

Dad Song

Why do you hurt me, something I said?
Scared and unhappy, something we shared?

Can't understand you, what's in your head?
Look how I'm bleeding, try to repair . . .

Look at you speaking, hiding the pain.
Why don't you say it? Crying again.

Hugging each other, going our way.
Wish we could talk, but scared, must contain.

Malcolm Nadeau, 18

Dad Song

Am I Going to Abuse My Kids?

The thick leather thing struck down at about 70 kilometers an hour from the force of my father's biceps — making contact with my 13-year-old brother's soft and gentle skin. Red blood cells almost reached the surface of the skin, making it red for the next half hour. Then the leather thing made contact with other parts of his body — five or six times. His muscles weren't strong enough to push against the heavy wooden door to keep his attacker out.

Knowing I'd be next, I tried to end the ferocious beating by a predator who doesn't even know what's happening to his helpless victim. I was able to distract my father from disciplining my brother the wrong way. He turned around, looking at me with an angry face and frightening eyes. His eyebrows formed a steep slope pointing to the top of his nose. It gave me an impression — a message — asking me what on earth I was doing. The Striking Force came on to me. It would not stop until the leather came face to face with my body seven or eight times.

Due to the amount of respect and fear we had for him, neither me nor my brother could have done anything about it.

This is an example of incidents that happened throughout my life since I was four or five. This is what introduced me to and taught me violence. It has taught me to be violent at any time there is an argument or a problem. This has been a major factor contributing to violence. This causes children to express themselves in a violent way.

Every time I think about my future I ask myself, "Am I going to abuse my kids?"

Mohammed Mosadeq, 15

Am I Going to Abuse My Kids?

I've Always Wondered

When is he finally going to realize that it's wrong. All it's creating is anger, pain, and fear. As soon as he comes home he starts swearing that my shoes aren't in the right place. The only reason I put my shoes in the right place from then on is because of the fear, not because I'm disciplined that way. Why do I have to live with all that fear, even at the age of 15? Damn it, I can't be that prince they've always dreamed of.

Can't he see the anger inside of me ready to explode? How, or should I, express all that anger. Whenever I get a chance on someone I will. But why should I live with all that anger? When do I get to wear a smile? I've always wondered how it would be to live free, without the furious anger, when I wouldn't have to.

Mohammed Mosadeq, 15

I've Always Wondered

Locked Up

I'm writing this because I wanna tell you you're driving me insane. I'm trying to make you understand that, even though you're not going to listen. I want you to give me a chance, I want you to stop using me as your punching bag. It's not my fault, it really isn't. You're the one who thinks I'm so bad, you twist everything around and make me guilty of everything. I want you to understand that you can't keep me locked up in this house all the time. I'm going crazy. I'm like a rat stuck in a hole doing nothing. How could you do this to me? I need friends, I need to have fun. I need to be able to go out. I need freedom.

Anonymous, 17

Locked Up

No one ever paid any attention to my thoughts.

PHOTO AND CAPTION BY JEREMY DUCHARME

The Wonders of Life

The pain going through my head
I can't take it anymore
The screaming, the crying, all the voices
Yelling out, making me cry with anger
Destroying everything in sight
I can't take it anymore
Sometimes I wonder why I was born
Why do I have a life?

Teniesha Ochrym, 15

The Wonders of Life

We all need someone to trust.

PHOTO BY COLLEEN WILSON / CAPTION BY SAIMA BAIG

I Remember

I remember the first time I saw Alanis live.
I remember when I was asked to be a godmother.
I remember begging my mother to have my dog stuffed after it died.
I remember biting my little cousin on the cheek.
I remember the stinging sensation of being hit.
I remember the first time I felt completely powerless.
I remember my stuffed bear that comforted me and soaked up all my tears.
I remember the lump in my throat that choked me when I wasn't allowed to cry.
I remember the first time I stepped into a courtroom.
I remember the smell of alcohol being camouflaged by cinnamon gum.
I remember the salty taste of blood.
I remember the searing pain of being burned with a cigarette.
I remember comforting my little sister when she was scared.
I don't want to remember anymore.

Amanda Stillemunkes, 17

Kind of Unnatural

I takes awhile to realize that your family is dysfunctional! Sometimes you can never even come to realize it. But families change, right? WRONG. Not unless they recognize it and even if they do they still have to make actions to change their attitudes and behaviour.

My family was like that but when we came to realize it unfortunately it was too late.

It's amazing how young kids go through so much. The only time of peace is at night when you're dreaming and even that was odd.

At the age of 5, I was a victim of violence, drugs, and alcohol abuse. Sure, it seemed all natural but that's the way I was brought up. I had a whole bunch of illegal substances in my midst and didn't even know. As I was getting older my parents supported their habits more than their four young kids.

As an individual I was offered anything I wanted, whether it was right or wrong. At the age of 5 my mother offered me a pull of her cigarette and I've been drinking beer ever since the age of 6. Kind of unnatural huh. Surprisingly I never got drunk or sick. But my dad, that was a different case. I always knew when my dad returned home from the pool hall. That's because it was the only time I'd hear my mom cry.

As I got older things got worse. Everyone got involved, the school, family services, police officers, social workers, and people I didn't even know existed. My life was being played with and my future was at stake. We were forced out of our home and were to have no contact with our mom. We lived with teachers, aunts, and grandparents.

My parents were tried for child abuse and lost their precious babies. After a month or two social services gave my mom a second chance! Hey, why not? The best of men can make a mistake. But as suspected she took advantage of the situation and did not change her ways.

My baby brother, who at the time was 7, was left to find cocaine and heroin in the bathroom cupboard. He didn't know any better than to give it to the cops that had come to check up on us.

Luck, I think not. But after that point was there any hope for me, my brother and sisters. Only God could have answered that question.

Kind of Unnatural

Anonymous, 16

To help children feel secure, you have to feel secure yourself.

PHOTO AND CAPTION BY EVE HILL

I believe that every child on this earth is brought down as an angel.

PHOTO BY SHERRI-LYNN BURGESS / CAPTION BY SAIMA BAIG

Out of This Evil

For life can't offer things. You've got to give to receive. But sometimes you don't receive as much as you give. What do I mean by that? I mean life's not as good to you as it is to someone else.

The promise of a good home is not always true! Young child in his room listening to his parents fighting, feeling weak and alone, wishing to be out of this evil. His father whips his mother and then kicking her. She gets mad, but hopeless as her daily routine comes in passes. Evil coming upon his father. He then finishes his job. It's now his turn to be given a lesson of endless respect of a crazy father.

Out of This Evil

Anonymous, 15

Powerless

When a kid gets stabbed for his jacket or for money near
my house, why do I still live here?

A mother kills her child and a father rapes his daughter.
Why?

Kids smash in an old husband and wife's head in the
west, and car bombs kill bystanders in the east.

I can't do anything. Why.

I'm powerless.

Powerless

Jesse Sicinski, 14

Our city is condemned by a plague we cannot understand.

PHOTO BY SAIMA BAIG / CAPTION BY JEREMY DUCHARME

From Nova Scotia to Montreal

When I was about 2 or 3 years old, I was living in Nova Scotia with my mom. My dad left us alone with my sister who was 7 years old. My mom, after a while, met this man who seemed nice and treated us like his daughters.

So we moved to Montreal. From all I can remember growing up it seemed nice. He was kind and sincere and the father-figure I never had.

But after a while the niceness didn't seem that nice. He started being mean towards my mother, calling her names and never letting her go out. We lost contact of our family in other places.

He started beating my mother a lot. It's something I try to forget.

One time will always stay in my mind. They were arguing. I was 7 and he punched her in the face so hard that she passed out. She was sent to the hospital and my mom was in critical condition for two weeks because she was pregnant at the time with my baby sister.

After a few years he left. He left only me and my three younger sisters alone. But my memory didn't leave my mind.

Melissa Colley, 16

From Nova Scotia to Montreal

They don't realize the down side to their Saturday night. PHOTO AND CAPTION BY ROXANNE RYDER

Sara

Sara was much like every other 15-year-old girl. She had dreams, she had ambitions. She was basically average, with one exception. Sara was addicted to drugs. This is what caused her life to end so suddenly.

Knowing Sara since kindergarten, I am able to tell you that she wasn't always like that. She was actually a very sweet, shy little girl, always polite, never obnoxious, caring for everyone before herself.

I noticed the changes in Grade 5. Each week she would come to school with terrible bruises on her body, or face, or maybe an imprint of a hand on her arm. "What happened?" "I fell down the stairs," she would say or "I fell off my bike." Years later, when we were changing for gym, I saw that her entire back was cut up as if she had been whipped. When I asked her about it, the look she gave me was so distant, so unfeeling, so cold, I wondered if it was really her. She turned her back to me again and replied, "I was bad."

As the years progressed, Sara became more and more closed in, with the exception of when she was high. Then she was her old self again: laughing and carefree. One thing I admired was her total fearlessness of death. She once told me that she figured that death couldn't be much worse than life when her father beat her and her mother drank every day of the week.

For a year, I didn't see or hear from her until last May. I almost didn't recognize her until she ecstatically called out my name. With a squeal of joy, she ran to me and gave me a hug. Every 15 minutes, though, she'd disappear to the bathroom to sniff crack. Once she asked me if I wanted to come, but I said I wouldn't touch anything so harsh.

The last time I saw her was three days before her death. We went to a party together and she was so proud and excited to introduce me to all her friends. I felt out of place though. Everyone looked different, acted different, dressed different from the way I did. I felt as though I didn't belong.

I now guess that that is the way Sara felt at home and at school. I suspect that is the reason why she joined that group of people because they made her feel as though she belonged . . .

I regret leaving that night because that was the last time I was in contact with her. When her friend called to tell me she was dead, it was funny but I didn't cry. I felt the loss, but I couldn't really get the grip that one of my friends was dead and from something as stupid as a heroin overdose. But it was her life and it was her decision to do what she did.

Jessica MacAran, 15

Does Anyone Care?

I believe that every child on this earth is brought down as an angel. Yet there are so many out there who've had their innocence taken away, for whom hope is just another four letter word, and they strive for it. Strive to get out of the "secret" that Mommy or Daddy has told them to keep. A terrible secret that keeps them from enjoying their childhood.

If you bring a child up to believe that the world is cruel and uncaring, and beat him when he does wrong, then I ask you, were you not a child once? Did you not want to be loved? What makes you hate?

Look out of the eyes of your child. What do you see? A father and mother who you think do not love you, a world filled with enemies, a world in which love has no meaning, and in which hatred is a powerful thing!

Why are you looking away? Doesn't it hurt to know that your child is living your life! The life you always hated. The life that was put upon you!

Don't you care? Doesn't anyone care?

Saima Baig, 19

Does Anyone Care?

There aren't many things out there that give kids a positive direction.

PHOTO BY TIFFANY PAYETTE / CAPTION BY JONAH ASPLER

I don't want to remember anymore.

PHOTO BY MALCOLM NADEAU / CAPTION BY AMANDA STILLEMUNKES

Why Did It Have to Happen?

I was so little at the time,
When you committed this awful crime.
It didn't have to turn out this way.
If only you had loved me the proper way
I'd still be with you today.

Why did it have to happen and why me?
You made it hard for me.
If only you could see.
Out of all the people in the world,
Why your daughter?
No matter what,
You should have been charged with manslaughter.

You probably think I'll forget about it
Later on in life.
If you think about it,
My memories will be full of strife.
I'd rather you be dead.
But they said you could live instead.
On your windows I hope you like bars,
Through them you'll see only stars.
You're like the pollution that's in the air
By screwing up someone's life, which isn't fair.

Why did you have to do this
And why me?
You were never a father to me
And you never will be.

Miranda Collins, 16

Why Did It
Have to Happen?

In the Name of Love

It was about a week before my birthday. I was on my ramp in front of my house with Mat. Mat was my world, my Romeo, my love, my everything. We were sitting cuddled up and looking at the sky, talking and just holding each other being happy.

The sky was dark and the stars were twinkling bright in the sky. There were people walking down the street but nothing seemed to matter. My cat was in the window staring as if he were staring at us. He had this look on his face as if he didn't want me to be there. I was so happy though that I didn't care.

We started talking about old relationships and old friends. All of a sudden his face, his face started to scrunch up and I don't even remember why he got upset. He shoved me and started screaming. All I could do was gawk, gawk at the fact that my boyfriend could do such a thing. He always bragged about how women should not be hit. Me believing very strongly about this decided to push him off me. He got so mad at me that he punched me and cracked my jaw. I should have walked right into my house, but no . . . Miss I think I'm a feminist but my boyfriend is beating the living crap out of me.

I started to cry and he told me he never wanted to see me again. Something came over me and I started chasing him and he grabbed me and shoved me into a wall and kicked me right in the shins. I fell to the ground and collapsed. Twenty minutes later he came back crying and telling me how much he loved me.

We went out for a year longer but that night I lost a piece of my soul and dignity but I guess it was all in the name of love . . . As if!

A broken jaw does not mean you love someone.

Judy Baser, 17

In the Name of Love

PHOTO BY JUSTIN FULLERTON

The Horror Still Remains

However much she runs from him
success will be postponed
sitting watching days go by
will turn her heart to stone.

However much she runs from him
he's always in her way
his iron fist takes full control
she cannot run astray.

However much she runs from him
her tears won't cease to flow
her thumping heart, her quivering hand
her fear begins to grow.

However much she runs from him
the horror still remains
like the story of a jailed bird
trying to break the tight restraints.

However much she runs from him
in the end it's all the same
the wounds are new, the flesh is raw
for him it's just a game.

Sarah Topey, 17

The Horror
Still Remains

It's hard to believe that it happened to me . . . Why me? PHOTO BY JESSE SICINSKI / CAPTION BY ANONYMOUS

A Part of Life

I don't remember the time it started or how old I was. All I remember is that it happened. I remember thinking "why me?" Why couldn't I be a normal little girl? That's all I wanted, but instead I grew up with a deep, dark secret.

In the beginning it didn't really affect me, but as I grew older I realized that what happened to me was wrong. I felt so naive I didn't even fight him off. I just lay there. I thought it was normal. You know what makes me feel dirty about it? The fact that he used to buy me candy afterwards. As my payment.

For most of my life I have managed to block it out. Once in a while I'll have a break down, but then I get back up on my feet again.

I only opened up to two people and it was very hard for me, but you know what? It happened to them too. I was so shocked! A lot of people that I know were sexually abused when they were younger. It's almost as though it's a regular thing. A part of life. It's usually done by someone you know.

My baby sitter was the culprit, and nothing was ever done about it. I don't remember what he looks like, and I'm glad.

Anonymous, 15

A Part of Life

Pricked

Pricked

He tears her hole wider
Explores up inside her
Ejaculates his poison
To give her life new reason.
She had a plea
And she would've been free
Had she found her voice
Now she has no choice.
In the hotel bed she lied
Her heart spread open wide
To the man she lay beside
Her life he denied.
She sold her soul that night
For her life she now must fight.
She has more important cares
Caused by the disease she now shares.
Half gone is her life
She will be no one's wife
She will be no one's mother
Not even anyone's lover
She is all by herself
No one to share the wealth
All she lost, never to be found
It will be buried with her in the ground.
All the moments she'll miss
All of them tossed into the abyss
But there is still a little hope
If only she can cope.
The few moments she has left to savour
Will give her blood some new flavour.
Still her end is in view
But she's just as good as you.

Colleen Wilson, 17

Is it ourselves or the circumstances we're born into that drive us into submission?

PHOTO AND CAPTION BY TESS VO

The Brand of the Devil

I am a woman with the brand of the devil on me. In fact, it's tattooed on my left breast. The man/animal who raped me tattooed my breast two weeks before he fornicated my 14-year-old virgin body, virgin soul.

All sorts of weird and sick things have happened to me since . . . and I am blind and numb to the harm that they cause me. That is a fault that I must repair because wounds need to heal and time is the bandage.

I've spoken to many rape victims and it's my observation that after they have experienced such a trauma, girls/women care much less about whom they share their bodies with. There is much less self-control and self-respect.

It's such a painful part of life to talk about. Some victims knew the person who did it, some were strangers. Some were raped by many men, some were raped by one.

But in every story I've heard, the woman went into shock, her soul separated from her body, being numb to the pain and trying to ignore the horror happening to her. Yet the minute it's over you take on shame, self-hatred, low self-esteem, and disgust as your new best friends.

These girls and women have a tendency to blame themselves for being there at the wrong place at the wrong time. You often hear, "If I had just . . ."

Then later, perhaps after having told a loving friend or an understanding family member about this emptying experience, hatred comes into the heart. A hatred so strong that, if it would have been present at the time of the rape, there is no way that the bastard's paws would have touched you.

This hatred, though, if not dealt with, will affect all relationships with males. To him it was just a great fuck . . . moments of pleasure while ruining innocence, trust, purity, and the beauty of lovemaking for a very, very long time.

Anonymous, 16

The Brand
of the Devil

The Stranger

Standing in the corner of an empty room, the tears stinging her eyes, she comes face to face with the stranger. He moves towards her. She knows what's coming next. He holds out his hand. But not to love and comfort her, only to hurt her. To take away her innocence. And when it's all over, she will sit in her corner, full of shame, rocking herself, trying to stop trembling. He has scarred her for life. Made her unpure. Made her have to live in fear. In those treacherous never-ending moments, he has put her in a secret hell forever. And when she buries her face in her hands, sobbing quietly to herself, she sees his face in her mind. And she realizes that he wasn't a stranger after all.

Amanda Stillemunkes, 17

The Stranger

Tonight's Sacrifice

The weakness of the day sets its minimal rays into the dark pub. I try a black beer in a beef to the calf glass. Two old hens at my left and one old man with an umbrella.

A Norwegian man who gets older to me after every drink he buys me. Buying my time, my feminine odour, my vulnerability. I make myself as strong as the last drink and fight off what's supposed to happen. He leads me around and I let him, pretending he's someone else. Telling him lies like when royalty needs to kill to get to the throne.

Drawn quickly to the same pub with the same smell except with a whole new pulse. I find the first table with a gorgeous redhead and sit facing him.

We go to a club and dance with our roots above ground, shaking the dirt everywhere. I am a giant tomato and everyone can see. My body temperature is making my eyes change colour. My shirt won't fit right, something pulls me outside. My redhead waits for a better time, but my time is NOW.

So I do the first redhead I see by the sea, my eyes as pale as the stones beyond the pier I endure and then he leaves me to dry with the concrete that feels wet. My back is a little scraped.

Back to the hostel and I'm ready for a shower. But all I can think about is that piano. Alone with a piano and a nice dress. The room is dim and my smell of sex is nearly forgotten with my song to ease tonight's sacrifice.

Tonight I took a taste I'd asked for dearly. A bit that was mistaken when I thought I was starving. Such a craving for me and yet here I am playing the same song. I outstretch my bare arms to soak in all notes played in a soft, violent, sorrowful way that invited in the air.

I cleared my throat and asked for a cigarette. He came right over and looked at me. I looked at him and still watching him watch me I studied him. The German and I are soulmates because he heard me in song.

Out behind the palace, enveloped in a fog I don't even know it. Ahead of me walk a few guys. One Dutchman becomes a redhead and I open my arms and breathe for his smile so wide. He catches my eye and smiles striking towards me with a drug.

In his touch and smell this man completely strange to me, his sperm on me, I self-destruct.

Meghann Delves, 18

Tonight's Sacrifice

It's Not the End

Arrived at the scene. It's 2:00 a.m. I heard the screaming and shouting.

Pushed the surrounding people aside for a shocking view. I got what I expected.

Call an ambulance, my friend's been shot. Don't move, brother, stay still, your family needs you.

Everybody get back. Blood's coming out of his mouth like tomato juice. The blood takes the stage again.

If you escape the darkness of this life, I'll get messed up.

With his last bit of energy he pointed to the tattoo on his neck.

Death is worth the respect. A volcano of blood expelled from the wounds on his chest.

Turned around, and the ambulance was there. There was nothing they could do.

It can't be, he's about to leave.

Finally, the struggle came to an end, he was pronounced dead.

But the story is not over.

Mohammed Mosadeq, 15

It's Not the End

It's a war we didn't start, but we're going to finish.

PHOTO AND CAPTION BY JEREMY DUCHARME

Downtown

Downtown

How can I explain myself? I was never one of those troublemaker kids who made a lot of noise or took things out of other people's back yards. I was always friendly, in earnest, and tried my best to be a good girl to everyone.

In high school I was a rebel, but not in that way. I didn't make too much noise or anything mostly smoking joints at recess and having a best friend who was the only boy in school wearing makeup. Like I said, never a bad kid. Teachers always failed me, but they never had anything bad to say, except that I was a daydreamer.

I always got along with my parents. My dad lived in a little one-room apartment. We would hang out until the blue hours of the morning. He'd say: "Here little sister, don't shed no tears." "No Woman, No Cry," it's always kind of been our song.

My mother was in a party stage too. We'd be at home tripping on acid and she'd say: "Walk around the block three times and then I'll give you some hash, that'll calm you down."

My parents always understood things that other people's didn't. That's why I can't understand how I got here.

I was going to do a B & E with no other intention but to get something to trade the turks for a couple of flaps. Now it takes a full point to take away the sickness.

I don't feel as though I'm addicted. I feel like I'm diseased. People shouldn't look at me like I'm a junkie. I've just got this illness. That's what heroin really is.

We used to always get so excited when we'd shoot smack all we'd need is 10 bucks each and a needle, and we'd be on the nod all night. I know plenty of junkies. My brother's a junkie.

Don't do it three days in a row, that was the big advice and we never did. Just once a month, twice a month, once a week, twice a week, every day and we never even noticed.

After a month, I realized what I'd done: I crossed the line from PCP and Coke and Pot. This was scary.

Heroin sounds very angry. All red and black and hot like hell or something.

That's when I found out. I lay in a bed in a hotel room in the States for four days sweating like a man, only to have it freeze on me when I'd run to the bathroom to vomit.

When you're coming down, the sickness is worse than any William Bourroughs perversion could explain. It's the most painful torture a human being can go through. Your body feels like it's trying to escape a body nylon that is two sizes too small and alternately freezing and boiling.

After four days, I came home and went back on the junk.

In my mind this is sufficient reason to break into someone's home and risk their lives and my freedom.

But you'll never feel it. You never jonesed before when the hospitals tell you to do more and the clinics don't give you more than three pills unless you sign the papers that let them look you up.

It's not a big stretch to take what you need.

Anonymous, 16

A Boy I Know

There is a boy I know who is surrounded by violence on a daily basis. It wasn't always this way. He grew up in a fairly normal family since both his parents are professionals. Then one day his mother fell into a deep depression and tried to kill herself by slitting her wrists. He found her, alive, in a pool of blood.

Naturally, this traumatized and confused the boy, who, in all his 12 years had never imagined that such a horrible thing could happen, let alone to his own mother. The boy changed dramatically after that, began taking drugs and drinking to hide and suppress his pain.

Eventually, the boy got so heavily involved with drugs that, when problems escalated at home, he ran away to another big city to do drug runs, thinking he was going to leave all his problems behind.

Once there, he took to living on the streets and, as a means of survival, he joined a gang to find safety in numbers. He saw many horrible things — muggings, killings, and gang fights — but since he was living it, he became adjusted to the violent life style.

Then one day, in an arcade, he and his gang had a confrontation with another gang. A knife was pulled on his best friend, and, knowing that if he didn't do something his friend would be killed, the boy took out a knife that he happened to have in his pocket. He stabbed the assailant, killed him, and then ran away, never looking back.

Eventually, the boy was arrested for drug trafficking, and brought back to Montreal to live in a group home. After a short stay, he went home to live with his parents and was left to resume his life as it had been, before he had seen and done all the horrible things.

But how could he be expected to function in everyday life, with so much pain and regret inside him, with no one knowing what he had done, no one to talk to? Almost inevitably, he picked up his frequent drug use, treating it as an anesthetic to numb his pain.

After a while, he was sent to rehabilitation, but remained sober only for two months after his release, because they were not treating the problem, but rather his solution, his way of escaping his problems.

Today, he hangs out in one of Montreal's worst neighborhoods, carrying around a lead-filled leather whip, a knife, and wearing steel-toed boots for protection. He claims to be the victim of or witness to several muggings and violent attacks each week, and feels he is only protecting himself from the inevitable.

It makes you wonder whether if maybe he had had someone to talk to from the start, some, or all, of this might never have happened.

A Boy I Know

Leana Satim, 16

There's no turning back. PHOTO AND CAPTION BY ANNA MARIA LOF

The Jacket

It was late at night when I lost my love, my best friend, my world. Clifford, a high-school drop-out who was trying to support his mother due to his father's death three weeks earlier, was on his way to his car to go home when he was brutally slaughtered.

When his body was found, he had been stabbed 16 times in and around the heart. His own mother could not even recognize him due to the bruises covering his face. She noticed that he wasn't wearing his jacket.

When I got the phone call, I felt as if my soul had been ripped out of me and sent to a far-off place where I could never find it again and I haven't, nor will I ever.

Eventually a confession was made. The perpetrator said, "I wanted his jacket. I didn't mean to kill him."

I cannot seem to understand why or how, but this is a problem in our society, and I will contribute all of myself and all within my power to make a difference.

Teria Delaportas, 18

The Jacket

Don't close your eyes to his cries of despair. PHOTO AND CAPTION BY JESSE SICINSKI

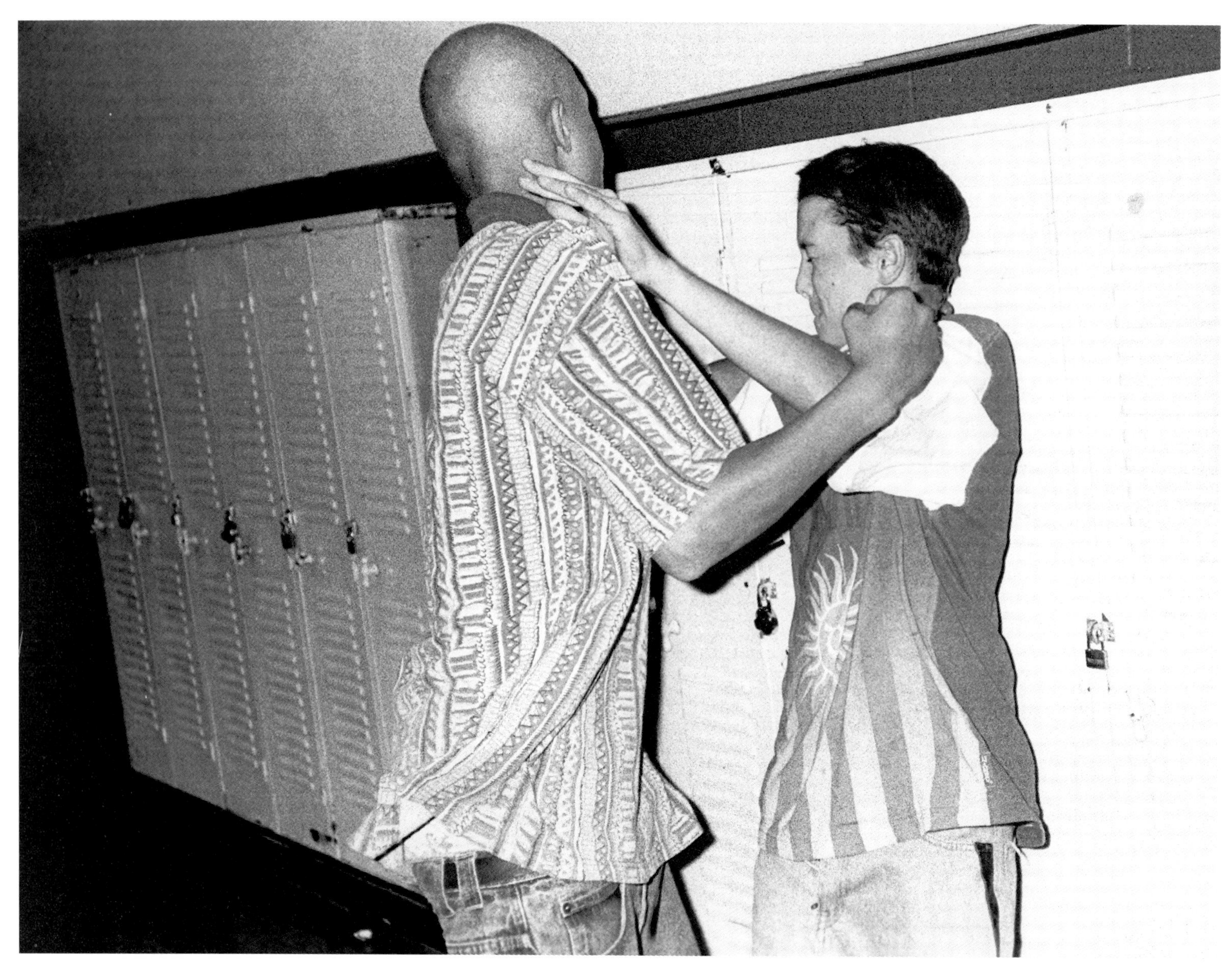

My adrenalin was pumping and I didn't want to stop. PHOTO BY JESSE SICINSKI / CAPTION BY JEREMY DUCHARME

First Fight

First Fight

My first fight was kind of an out of body experience with fists flying and the smashing of a fist against a face and screams which I'm not sure if they were mine or the other guy's. It was like I was more of a spectator than an actual combatant. I didn't feel any pain or remorse. I left the other guy lying on the ground curled up in a fetal position holding his bleeding nose and crying. After it was finished but later that night I felt guilty about how I left him. I began to feel my own pain. It felt as though my jaw had been ripped out and as though I had a punctured lung.

Danny Thorburn, 15

First Fight

Moving On

When I get angry, the best thing I can do is count to 10 or just walk away, but it wasn't always that way with me. In fact, it took the system three years to change my anger.

At first, I would express this poisonous anger by throwing some type of temper spasms, tossing things across a room or just, in general, with pure and unjustified violence.

The violence part of my anger was starting to get in the way, so I took up pot and beer and other toxins to keep off the violence.

So instead of destroying those prize possessions we own in life as a product of anger, I'd sit back and tilt my mind to a whole new realm and just forget about the world. It's so much easier than breaking everything in sight.

The thing is that you can't live your whole life nodding out here and there and running away from reality. You've got to be awake and alive.

And you will most definitely end up behind bars, walking around solving problems with your fists.

It's not worth it. Plus it's so much more relaxing just to move on.

Ian Berard, 18

Moving On

Where do we go from here?

PHOTO BY KRISTA LAJEUNESSE / CAPTION BY JESSE SICINSKI

There is only so much freedom. Then life screws you over.

PHOTO BY LEANA SATIM / CAPTION BY JAESON LEMAY

Free High

I can relate to boredom as a main factor for influencing youth crime. Not only boredom, but drugs and alcohol.

There have been many nights when me and my friends would get together and try to figure out what we could do to keep ourselves busy for the night.

Usually we would end up wanting to get high and/or drunk, but we never had any money for such things. So the main thing before getting intoxicated was to find money to do so.

Sometimes hours on end we would think about all the different ways to get this cash, and then narrow it down to the two or three crimes that were best suited for our current position. Most of the time we would be breaking and entering, robbing someone, or even just doing the good old fashioned "beer run."

Every night somehow, we would always get what we wanted, or should I say what we needed. And getting there with crime.

We were young, we weren't employed, our parents weren't rich — plain and simple. All we wanted to do was to fit in. All we wanted was to have fun, free of charge.

Bored alcoholics and druggies with no cash will lead to crime almost all the time.

I've changed. I know it's not worth all the hassle. But there's still a lot of people that don't know. And sadly enough, don't care.

Ian Berard, 18

Free High

The Red Line

THE DAY WAS HOT
THE DAY WAS DRAGGING
ONE SECOND CRAWLED LIKE
AN HOUR
IT DIDN'T TAKE LONG FOR THEM
TO GET
BORED.
IN SECONDS THEY FOUND
A DIVERSION.
IN SECONDS HE PULLED BACK
THE HAMMER.
IN SECONDS HE
PRESSED THE TRIGGER.
IN SECONDS HE
WATCHED AS
THE
RED
LIFE LINE
SLIPPED AWAY.
IN SECONDS HE WATCHED HIS OWN
BROTHER DIE.

THE DAY WAS HOT
THE DAY WAS DRAGGING
IT DIDN'T TAKE LONG TO
FIND
DADDY'S GUN
IT DIDN'T TAKE LONG FOR
THE DAY
TO END.

Junie Desil, 17

Weapons of frustration have no place in our lives.

PHOTO AND CAPTION BY EVE HILL

Teardrops of Blood

Teardrops of blood fall from the sky,
They slowly caress the side of my face
Leaving red streaks smeared against my cheeks.
The cold red drops of humanity destroy the barriers
And walls of my innermost emotional thoughts.

Like acid they burn through my chest
and pierce my heart like 1,000 hornets
Stinging my eyes, I see no longer.

Teardrops of blood ripple in the
Puddles of humanity, urging to be heard.
My clothes rest stained with blood
On the ground as I lie here naked
Crying my tears of blood.

Jesse Sicinski, 14

Teardrops of Blood

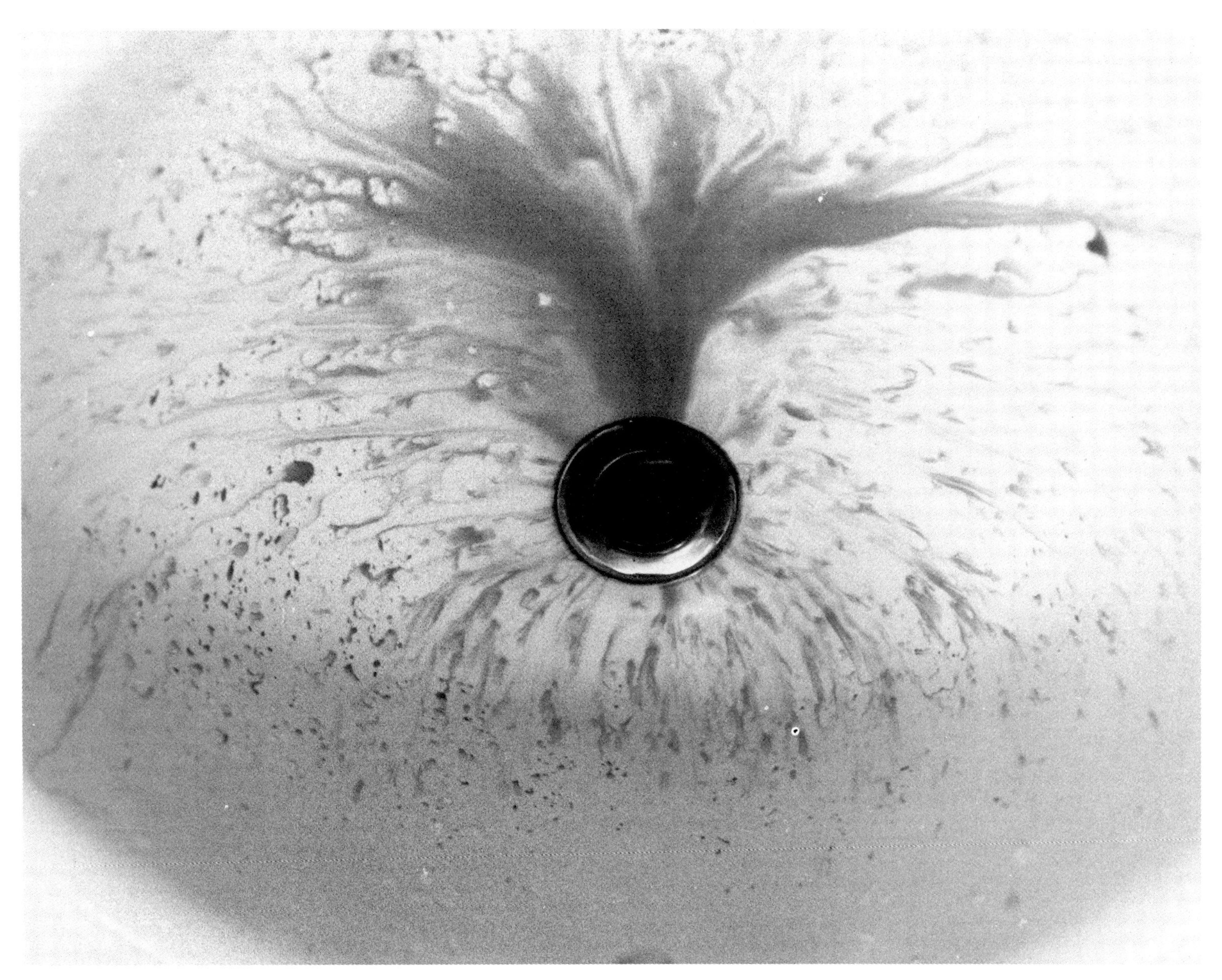

Photo by Nicholas Ramirez

Shattered Dreams

Why?

I can tell you why.
You think that I'm a simple, soft woman.
And I tell you I'm not.
Then you ask, Why?

And I answer you so
you can't understand!
"Instead of caring with my fist and my mouth,
I will care with my mind.
And show you why."

You asked, Why?
"You still don't understand,
So I will show you."
I will love and care for myself,
To turn the tables
and now you can ask, Why?

You say you love me.
Why?

You say you care.
Why?

You say you love me but you put me down.
Why?

You say you care but you still hit me.
Why?

You rule my life and tell me what to do.
Why?

You say if you leave me
I will kill myself.

Why?

Tabitha Cross, 17

Why?

Why don't you listen? Your voice covers your ears from what I have to say.
From what you should hear. A loner, no love, no comfort, no one who cares.
Only tears. I promised I wouldn't cry any more. It was time I stopped . . .
You think I'm disobedient, and rude, like I don't care. You think you screwed up,
but you didn't. All I need is love. A love you want. I need to know that someone needs me,
someone loves me, someone cares. You think you know me, but you don't.
You only know my predictable cover. A thick but breakable shell.

Heather Wright, 16

Just as long as there is a tomorrow, you know what you have to do to make life better. PHOTO AND CAPTION BY JENNEFER JENEI

Poor Old Man

People crying on the streets,
abused, drunk, doped-up,
no food to eat.
A little girl sees her daddy
beating her mommy and
all she asks is
"why?"
A poor old man
full of beer and liquor,
he looks at his wrinkled
hands and face, knowing that he has
no home, place, or shelter
to stay,
he puts out a hand,
for a nickel, quarter,
dime, or penny.
But still no one gives
him any.
He looks up in the sky,
and all he asks is,
"Why, God, why?"
One day the world will
have no more
"Whys?" and no more
cries on the streets.

Melissa Colley, 17

Poor Old Man

When do I get to wear a smile?

PHOTO BY NATISHA RYNER / CAPTION BY MOHAMMED MOSADEQ

Once a Person Is Lost

Once a person is lost, can they be found?
When a person can't talk, do they make a sound?
How important can one's life be?
There's something in life I just don't see.
There's no place to hide, no place to go.
My smile's a mask that covers a frown,
Emotions are rivers in which I could drown.
I can feel the struggle to keep aboard
And all strong efforts are lacking reward.
I can just imagine others like me,
Just about everyone wants to be free.
It's hard these days to relate to someone,
It feels like I'm alone under the sun.
But my question is "Does someone really care?"
I don't think so.
I wouldn't dare.

Eve Hill, 17

Once a Person Is Lost

What do I have to do to be noticed? PHOTO AND CAPTION BY TENIESHA OCHRYM

I can make a difference to the world, my community, and my soul.

PHOTO BY JULIA PAUL / CAPTION BY MELISSA COLLEY

Acceptance, Care, Love: Gangs

A group of teens walking down a street, any street. They have no definite plan except to roam the streets for a while, with weapons, with time on their hands. They're a gang.

In the gang they find acceptance, care, and love, which seems ironic, since in a gang you also find violence, heartbreak, and bloodshed. But it's true. Youths in gangs often find the love and acceptance they otherwise wouldn't find at home. The gang is like a family. It is a family. If a youth has to find love and acceptance in a gang, where otherwise they should find it in a family, shouldn't we be concerned? Shouldn't parents especially be concerned?

Junie Desil, 17

Acceptance, Care, Love: Gangs

The Miracle I Would Ask For

I lost the love of my life because of a drunken driver. Now the only memory I have of him is a mental picture of when the mortician closed his casket and when I read his eulogy.

The greatest and most precious gift he has ever given me was the gift of love. That is why I would want him back in this world. That is the miracle that I would ask for.

I'm thinking of you
again.
I do it often
mostly when I've been hurt inside,
but sometimes when I'm having
the most
fun.
Wishing you were here
Or wishing I were there.
Wishing anything that would mean
we'd still be together.

Anonymous, 17

The Miracle I Would Ask For

PHOTO BY COLLEEN WILSON

WALKSAFE
WALKSAFE
WALKSAFE

Fear

I don't want to be hurt again, so I
fear love.
I don't want to be let down again, so I
fear friendship.
I don't want disappointment again, so I
fear life.
I don't want to be alone again, so I
fear hate.
I don't want to be a victim again, so I
fear violence.
I don't want to be forgotten, so I
fear death.

Were we put on this planet to live our
lives in fear?
The fear of love,
the fear of friendship,
the fear of life.
The fear of hate,
the fear of violence,
the fear of death.
We all live our lives in fear.

Miranda Collins, 16

The gun went off and I was running and yelling out my brother's name.
PHOTO BY ANONYMOUS / CAPTION BY MELISSA SAMUEL

I Can't Wait for It to Shine . . .

As the sun goes,
the darkness rises upon
my soul.
As I hide in the darkness I can still
hear the cries of sadness through the
walls.
As the sun rises, the flowers bloom again.
The river and the lakes are calm now.
The walls are open, nothing can stop
me from leaving, but the darkness
which lies on the otherside.
As the darkness begins to rise,
I can see the happiness of
my day start to die.

Patrick LaPointe, 17

I Can't Wait
for It to Shine . . .

It's the place where I put the scattered pieces of my life together and together again.

PHOTO BY MALCOLM NADEAU / CAPTION BY ANONYMOUS

Unwanted

Unwanted

Nobody talks to me,
Nobody listens to me,
Nobody loves me,
Nobody cares about me.

I could die and no one would cry.
I could run away and no one would do anything.
I could hide in my room and no one would notice.
I could disappear and no one would care.

Maybe I'll drop out of school.
Maybe I'll get pregnant.
Maybe I'll do drugs.
Maybe I'll live on the streets.

I never feel wanted.
I never feel loved.
I never feel happy.
I never feel anything but unwanted.

Should a child live like this?
Should a child feel like this?
Why don't you tell me
because I live and feel like this.

Unwanted

Miranda Collins, 16

I am lost in this unforsakeable, lonely and distraught world! PHOTO BY SAIMA BAIG / CAPTION BY ANONYMOUS

I'm not the only person who has thought about suicide. PHOTO BY JEREMY DUCHARME / CAPTION BY ANONYMOUS

Sucks

Searching for happiness is a journey
forever
Running around aimless — three blind mice,
Wasted youth and a fistful of ideas
I had a young and optimistic point of view.
It's a long fall from heaven,
No one's there to catch you,
Brace yourself.

Gabriel Cukier, 15

Sucks

Photo by Semira Weiss

Transparent

You say you'll always love me,
Until the end of time.
You never want to talk to me,
Your love is such a crime.

I'm on the edge of an ocean,
The air smells like violence and hate.
I might jump to show you,
Your love came way too late.

I can't even talk to you,
Because you don't understand.
And when I do try,
You raise your hand.

Either you're at work or with your boyfriend,
And I know you think I am errant.
You don't even see me,
It's as if I am transparent.

Miranda Collins, 16

Transparent

Shattered Dreams

Life starts off with a simple dream. Before you know it, your dream breaks slowly. Piece by piece, it falls to the ground. Then, before you know it, you're standing in a daze, with no one to mend your broken pieces together.

Ryan Dwyer, 18

Shattered Dreams

Regret

As the cold hard steel bites my wrists with awakening clicks and pinches, I realize that what I've done is wrong.

But that's not enough, not enough for the big men in blue as they remind me of unstoppable and all-powerful gods, leading me towards what all my thoughts go against. A door. A door like no door seen on any ordinary street or in a hallway, but a door of great strength, driving hopeless thoughts into my mind.

As I enter the room behind the door, I'm struck by the frosty draft driving goosebumps up and down my body. Then, with a shuddering clack of steel, I'm no more a free man and all I can do is stare into the blinding light overhead that drills into my eyes, burning them awake, forever.

I don't like this place, this place of evil, this place of sorrow, this place of total darkness, darkness of the soul and mind as you sit and await the outcome of your misfortune.

Regret

Ian Berard, 18

Photo by Junie Desil

Evil

I can't really see it, it's like a blur. I see flashes then it fades and I can't see a clear picture. I can't touch it, but I know it's there because I can taste the malice, the hatred. Most of all, the bitterness and revenge. Why is it coming back?

I can smell the rotting decaying as it goes deeper. It grasps your heart deep, deep inside. Then slowly it creeps up and destroys.

You don't realize what's happening. It takes you over. You are overcome by hate and revenge. There is no light at the end of the tunnel. There are just two things waiting there for you. When you're born, you don't have a choice. You're born with the evil planted in you.

But how can you think there is no hope? How did you get here? Did you just appear? If so, there is no purpose for your life. There isn't any order. You can kill and there is no consequence.

Why would there be love *and* hate if there is no difference between us and the animals?

Heather Wright, 15

The supersonic space pony killed the little prince. PHOTO AND CAPTION BY JESSIE SICINSKI

Determination Day

The day will come.
The day when the leaves of the roses will fall,
When angels are too tired,
When love has the desire to hate.
Hope will dissolve in the ultimate cloud of death.
Death will become a dictator.
It's the day the world will rest — not in peace but in riot.
The wicked will win.
Who will save you then?
Your killer toys?
Not your illusions of god!
Nothing . . .

Mohammed Mosadeq, 15

Determination Day

PHOTO BY DIEDERIK MUYLWYK

PHOTO BY DANNY THORBURN

Erosion

Voice of anguish for a generation
The raw screams of pain
Echo throughout the vast auditorium
Agony carried throughout your youth
Hell to you is no longer unknown
Surviving death and years of fear
The angel flies overhead
His memories, clear and vivid
To you it's not so far away
The once precious jewel now eroded
Music playing for an empty room
The coldness burns your heart
The ones who hate you, give you what you want
The ones who love you, leave you here

Colleen Wilson, 17

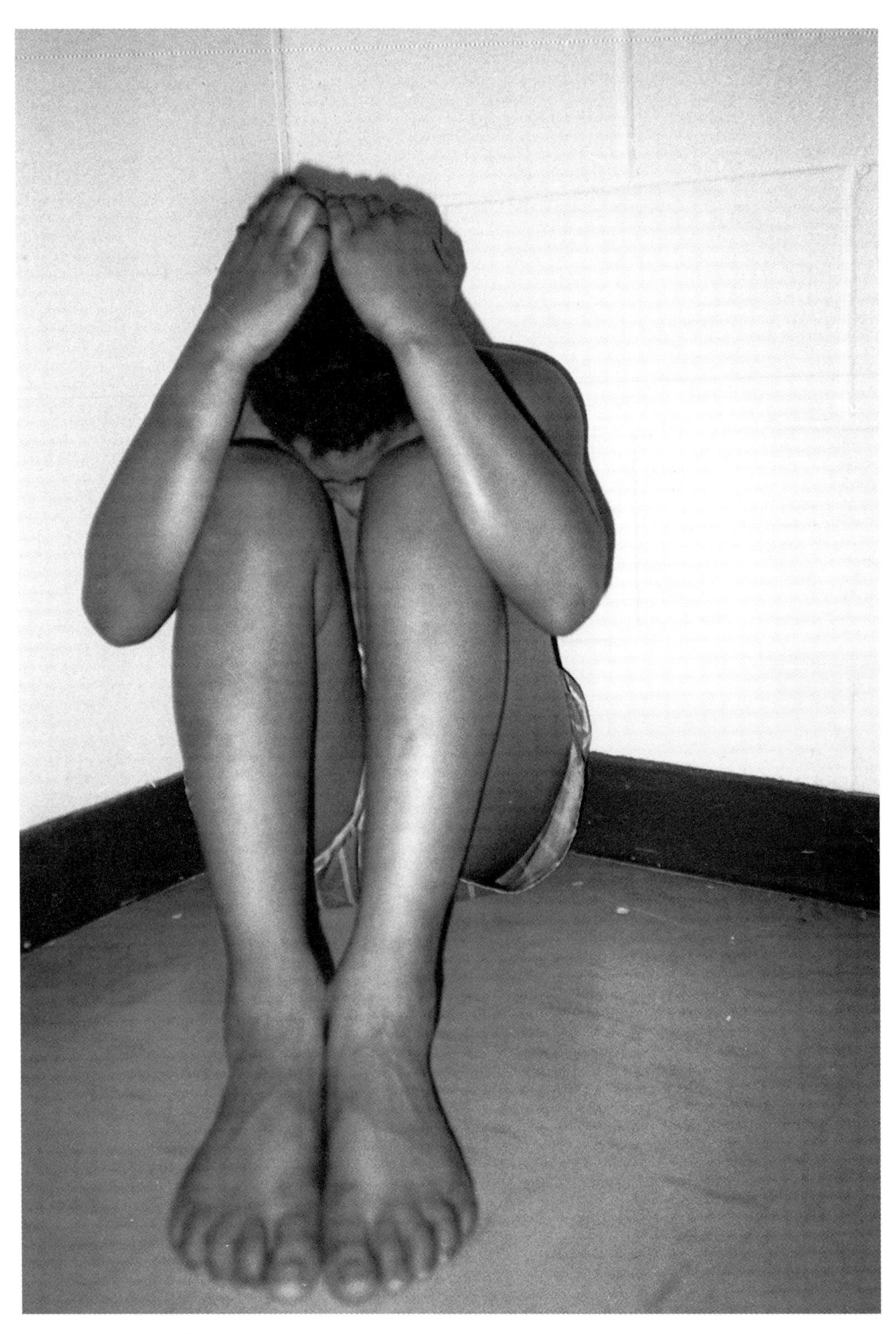

You cannot hide from your problems. They'll never leave you until you face them. PHOTO AND CAPTION BY TENIESHA OCHRYM

Ugly

I hate what I see, and who that person is. Her ponytail is too oily, her face is too ugly, and her feet are too big. She hears others judging her, she shakes their laughter off and becomes more the emotionless child she dreams of, and cries in a lonely corner. No love has been given to her, and she gives none to others. Who knows what she thinks of me or of what she sees. I hate her so much but I also want to hold her so she will feel safe. And then I realize she is me looking in a mirror.

Naomi Dylan, 14

She sits on the subway, saying she doesn't care, but her makeup can't hide her sadness.

PHOTO AND CAPTION BY MOHAMMED MOSADEQ

Making All the Decisions

All alone making all the decisions . . .

No help from the one I love. He says, "Oh, I'll get a job, I'll take care of you and the baby."

It's like waiting for a miracle to happen, and as they say, "A watched pot never boils."

I tell myself I don't need him, I can do better or I can do it on my own. But deep down inside I think so much differently.

All alone making all the decisions . . .

He says, "I'm coming to see my woman tonight." But oops, he bumps into a friend, "I'm sorry baby, I got drunk." I say to him, "What? You got too drunk to call?"

I mean, what's gonna happen when his baby comes? Is he gonna say, "I'm sorry son, I bumped into a friend and got too drunk to come and see you?"

I don't want the same lifestyle for my child as I lived. I want so much more. If I have to do it on my own, without him, then I will. I will love and give to this child unconditionally, but MY LOVE can only go so far.

All alone making all the decisions . . .

Can't say that I didn't try, because I tried a lot.

I tried so much that I cry myself to sleep. When does the hurting stop? I don't think it ever will.

"Whichever way it turns out," I say to myself, "don't think negatively, you're not that kind of person, you'll do the best whether it be two or one. You've tried and that's all you can do, besides being strong."

All alone making all the decisions . . .

Kate Martin, 19

Making All the Decisions

Alone

They shout,
She cries.
They call her names,
She cries.
No one knows why.

She goes to school
and puts on a show,
They think she's happy
but nobody knows.

She goes back home
and feels so low
and all alone.
Nobody knows.

It's time for bed,
and
nobody knows.
Nobody knows.
Nobody knows.

Sabrina Smith, 17

Once a person is lost, can they be found?

PHOTO BY JONAH ASPLER / CAPTION BY EVE HILL

Even the widest of open spaces won't free me from the prison that is my mind.

PHOTO AND CAPTION BY DIEDERIK MUYLWYK

My Secret Spot

My secret spot at Shawbridge was my dark, small closet. I went into my closet because I wanted room to breathe. I had a flashlight taped to the clothing bar (upside down) so I could read. By this I mean that when the lights were out that three-foot-square place was a room of no boundaries.

I couldn't see the walls, so they went on forever. In this room, I found solitude. No one pestered me except my thoughts. The staff left me alone because I would get pissed off if I was bothered.

I have always liked to be alone, mainly because I have been alone most of my life. No one ever really paid any attention to my thoughts. They only paid attention to my actions, be they legal or not. I was the only one who understood my complex way of thinking. And being in my dark, warm closet left me and my colourful thinking to myself.

So leave me alone!

Jeremy Ducharme, 18

Different

I came here and I didn't let any of you in,
But now I see that I was cheated.
I wore your uniform, I played your game,
But now I see that I was different
and you all hated it so.
You tried so hard to put me down,
to sink my ship.
I was the victim and you are superficial
But I will never blame any of you.
I know small things and I said very few words
And they slurred.
But you can't stand to see something
different.
You are afraid to look at each other.
You see through each other
and you are nothing anymore.
What you see that you don't even know,
you hate.
My truth is not a lie to me,
but it upsets you.
You hate because you don't even know who you are,
but I feel no sympathy.
I know who I am.
And I like what I see and you hate that,
therefore you hate me.

Different

Meghann Delves, 18

Sports bulletin board, Jarvis Collegiate Institute. PHOTO BY DIEDERIK MUYLWYK

The Street Kid

The girl only knew death in that lonely alley, where others had known theirs.

What kind of life can a street kid lead when nobody cares, nobody listens, nobody can see you?

Once she was in a gang, where she became no longer Sarah, but a drone.

Her mother would have loved her but she passed on, and her father was a block towards her.

All she had was her looks and her tough jacket.

You would ask about her friends but where were they, those nights she cried herself to sleep?

In the end, her life never touched anyone except the policemen who witnessed her death, and more kids dead in the street.

She was born Sarah but died as Room 213, number 2461001. Another death.

Naomi Dylan, 14

Some young people don't know what direction they want to go in. As long as they stick to the right path, they can go anywhere.

PHOTO AND CAPTION BY ROBERT ROBBINS

I Can’t Wait for It to Shine

Peace and love may be dead, but there is always hope.

Photo by Omar Williams / Caption by Nicholas Ramirez

PHOTO BY AMANDA STILLEMUNKES

A Helping Hand

DON'T SMACK THE SMILE
I PRODUCED FOR YOU ESPECIALLY
IT'S ONLY TO CHEER YOU UP BECAUSE YOU LOOK SO GLUM.
DON'T PUSH A HELPING HAND AWAY
FOR I STRAIN OUT MY ARM FOR YOU.
DON'T HANG UP YOUR PHONE
MY EARS ARE ON THE OTHER LINE WAITING TO LISTEN.
DON'T BE SO QUICK TO SHUT YOUR DOOR
BECAUSE I'LL NOT BE HERE FOR YOU NO MORE.

Jennefer Jenei, 16

A Helping Hand

Live Every Day to the Fullest

That is something we all have to keep in mind. 'Cause you never know when your time has come. In today's society you have to be careful about what you say. If you say the wrong thing to the wrong person, you can die.

Too many people these days are trigger happy. Unfortunately, Montreal is becoming worse each year. Some people don't realize how dangerous things are getting. But the truth is that those kind of people are just narrow-minded. If things keep on getting worse, where will the next generation end up?

You have to think about our kids. What kind of world do you want your child to grow in?

Try. You've got to keep the faith. Some day we can make it happen.

Make a difference, make the future. Make it possible for our children to grow up in a safe environment.

Anna Maria Lof, 17

Live Every Day
to the Fullest

Don't smack the smile I produced for you especially. PHOTO BY MATTHEW WOOLCOCK / CAPTION BY JENNEFER JENEI

Sometimes

Sometimes
I ask myself why I was born. Was I a mistake?
I tell myself "NO" don't think like that.
Sometimes
I say that I have no reason to live, that I should kill myself.
I tell myself "NO" don't think like that.
Because I'm born now, it's no mistake.
So I won't kill myself, 'cause I do have a reason to live.
For tomorrow, a brand new day.

Teniesha Ochrym, 15

Sometimes
Sometimes

Photo by Anonymous

Photo by Heather Wright

Yes!

I walk through my neighborhood; everyone says "hi!" I walk by a black boy and a white boy playing together. The neighborhood rings with laughter. I stop at a friend's house and enter without knocking. She greets me warmly.

After visiting I leave to catch the bus. I miss it. A complete stranger drives by and offers me a ride. I accept it.

Rewind . . . A complete stranger offers me a ride. I accept it.

OOPS! Did I forget to mention that this is a utopian society?

Unfortunately, this society exists only in my own mind.

In a society where almost every problem is solved through violence, it is these dreams which keep our hopes for a better world alive.

Junie Desil, 17

Yes!

Recovery

Since I've experienced violence of every medium possible,
and learned some of the secrets of the universe,
I've been able to distinguish between abusive situations and powerful, good ones.
I've learned to become a stronger person, knowing what I truly value — productivity, having a task, cleaning my backyard, cleaning my mind, my body, and my soul.

It's been a huge rollercoaster ride, stepping off of it by being detached from single events. Whether good or bad, I don't indulge in them. I've been able, through back-up resources such as books, articles, other people, to foresee danger, the potential for someone to be obsessive, violent. I now have a critical mind.

I've been sexually abused,
I've been mentally abused,
I've been verbally abused (discrimination, judged),
I've been physically abused (fights, rape).

I am not alone,
and this reassures me that life goes on.

I've been sexually abused so many times that there's still more I need to deal with about sex and feelings about sex.
But I'm no longer lost in my thoughts,
and I'm using my clarity as a tool to help others and help myself.

I am incapable of expressing myself verbally as much as I'd like to.
My physique has recovered, but I smoke cigarettes so I induce self-destructiveness.

All abuse roots from fundamental
problems that haven't
been properly dealt with.

Semira Weiss, 17

Recovery

We walk the same way but leave very different tracks.

PHOTO AND CAPTION BY ANGELA NEWBY

Loss

Part One/September to December
Life is at an end
I've lost a lot of friends
My mind has been numbed
All because I'm dumb.
My addictions have divided my soul
With great big empty holes.
No chance for goodbyes
All through my very eyes
My dad was taken away
Quickly in a final way.
I'll mourn them all
Yet I'll stand tall
Gives me a heartache
But cures my headache.

Part Two/January to now
My mother has come home to me
All is so clear for my eyes to see
Denial has pushed down all my problems
I remember how I used to ignore them
Success and recovery is a long, windy road
But as I look at my feet, I see it's made of gold
It seems like contemplating is all I do
But hopefully my life will come through.
In life I would love to use my talents
and maybe even be a parent
But whatever happens to me
I know I'll always have my family
And as for my mother
I hope that she will always know that I love her
No matter what.

Anonymous, 14

Within every tear of sadness there lies a grain of beauty.

PHOTO AND CAPTION BY DIEDERIK MUYLWYK

People say family violence is passed down from generation to generation, but that's no excuse. PHOTO BY JAESON LEMAY / CAPTION BY PHILIPPE MARTINS

To Parents of a Troubled Teen

Dear Mom, Dear Dad:

I wish you'd pay attention to him. Not when he gets into a fight. Not when the principal calls you. I wish you'd praise him for every good thing, however little, instead of harping on the bad. Instead of asking "What did you do now?" in resignation, ask him "How was your day?"

Don't criticize him, Mom. Don't yell at him, Dad. His self-esteem is fragile. He's sensitive, and he just wants your understanding and support. Don't harp on the failures in his report card. Praise him for his C's and D's.

Don't close your ears or your heart to his cries of despair. Don't let him shut himself from you, and don't give up. Don't ever give up.

Junie Desil, 17

To Parents of
a Troubled Teen

I drink life as it comes to deal with what I have swallowed emotionally.

PHOTO AND CAPTION BY AMANDA STILLEMUNKES

A Good Trick to Heal

When the end of a family comes from the bottom of a bottle, it's the worst feeling in the world.

The innocent world you had crashes down upon you, leaving you with left-over emotions, scared, depressed, alone, angry.

You feel like you're in your own world, alone, trying to find out what went wrong or when did it go wrong. That's all you think about.

But a good trick to heal is to occupy your mind. Find something you love, and all you eventually think about is what you love. Eventually your pain and thoughts will go away. Also, knowing that there are people who are willing to help . . .

Anonymous, 14

A Good Trick to Heal

Role Models

There are a lot of role models in my life. All of my friends in my church are my role models. They are extremely encouraging because when I'm down in the dumps they not only take the time to listen, but they lift me up in prayer. A lot of the time they shed new light on my dimly lit situation. For example, if I was talking to my mom and she started saying things like, "You made up stories about your dad sexually assaulting you. He would never do anything like that," my friends would say, "It's not your fault. Your mom is in a difficult situation and she is not ready to see how you've grown up and how much stability you now have in your life." When I hear that, I'm encouraged to keep going and not give up.

Sherri-Lynn Burgess, 18

Role Models

I'm Sorry

I always disappoint you,
I never do anything right.
This is how you made me feel,
while yelling at me last night.

I'm sorry for all those times,
I got brought home by the cops.
You're really mad at me,
and you hope that it stops.

I'm not even close to
what you want me to be.
I know that I'll change,
just you wait and see.

I'm sorry for all those times
when I ran away.
The first time should have been forever,
and now I have hell to pay.

You don't understand me,
and I don't understand you.
I just wanted to say I'm sorry,
and that much is true.

I hope you can forgive me,
and forget about the past.
Only this time I want
our relationship to last.

I'm sorry.

I'm Sorry

Miranda Collins, 16

I guess I was at the wrong place at the wrong time. PHOTO BY MELISSA COLLEY

My Story

As I prepare to tell this story, my mind reflects on how different my life is now. Simple things please me, and my safety is assured. I trust less and smile more.

I am 16 years old. Now, I get good grades, stay away from drugs, and give people my seat on the bus.

But after you read this you will wonder: how do I still smile?

You see, four years ago, I ran away from home and lived on the streets.

Two years ago, I entered Alcoholics Anonymous.

One year ago, I entered a youth protection group home.

In October, I found out that my mother is dying from multiple sclerosis.

I have surely seen more horrors that the average 16-year-old.

I remember all the times I wanted to die, to pull the trigger, open the bottle of pills and swallow them, jump off the building on the side street in Old Montreal. Anything to ease the pain. I was convinced it would never get better, that nothing would ever change.

I guess I should start at the beginning, where it started to go wrong. I had a lot of dreams, a lot of hopes, and I still do, but they are different hopes now. I was 11 when my mother first started getting sick. She went to countless doctors, neurologists, regular doctors, psychologists, you name it. We watched her slowly deteriorate; this strong, funny woman, who always had a joke to tell and time for her daughters and son, started to become someone I didn't even know.

I was also 11 when I took my first drink.

Now I know it was all connected, that it wasn't my fault, it wasn't anyone's fault. I had had my mother torn away from me by a disease that controlled her, and

a sister who, being the oldest, automatically became the head of the house, and — to this day — my worst enemy. To list the things we went through with her would take up a chapter in a book.

Sometimes I still feel hopeless, and like nothing is going to go right. But then I put it in perspective. And I work out my fears and pain instead of drowning them in Southern Comfort.

Sometimes it's hard to do. It takes all my strength not to reach for my purse and run to the Societé de Alcool de Québec. And they don't even care if I'm 16 years old or not. They'd sell it to me anyway. But I still don't do it. Because I have things, responsibilities to consider, people who would be disappointed in me. I would be disappointed in me.

I've always been very close to my mother. She made a great difference in the stages of my maturity. I believe I only began to grow up when I was 15, and decided to stop drinking and abusing drugs, and really started listening to my mom.

Soon, I will be starting a new life — leaving the group home, getting my own apartment, graduating, going to CEGEP.

I will be independent. I will have to answer to myself, if I come home late, forget to do homework, or even worse.

Drink.

Anonymous, 16

Back and forth, back and forth, I soared like an angel . . . No more despair.

PHOTO BY JULIA PAUL / CAPTION BY HEATHER WRIGHT

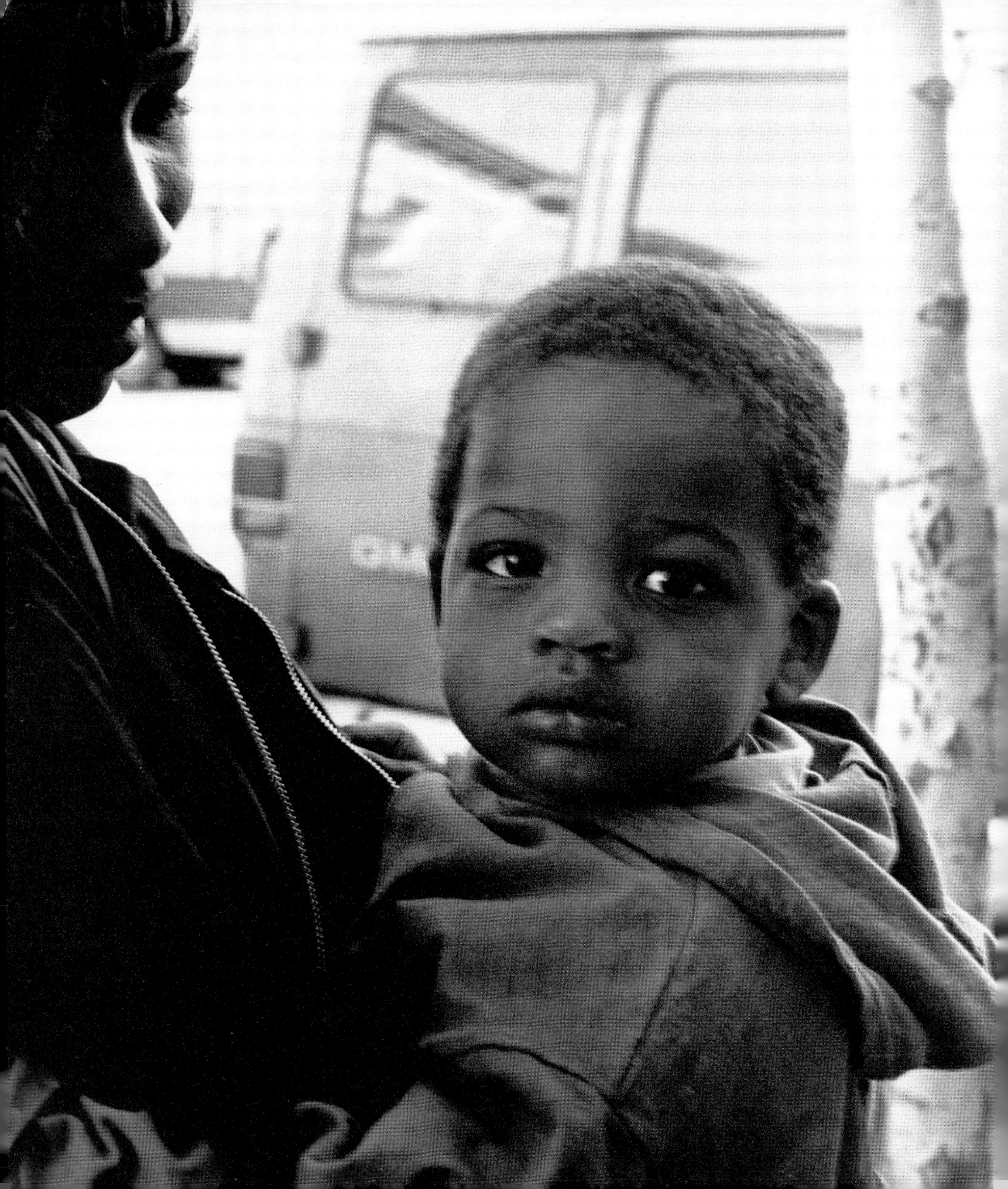

My Favourite Place

I love my mother's house because this is where I always, no matter what, feel comfortable.

I don't live with my mom, but we still maintain a strong relationship. I love being around her because she is neat, she understands me, she knows when something is wrong, and likes everything I like.

So I have no other choice than wanting to be around her more than any other person.

My Favourite Place

My Mom's House

A very good memory that sticks in my mind is the last time I went to Ottawa with my sister to visit my mom and older sister for Christmas. I love Christmas, I love my mom's house, and I love my mom most of all. You could say I was with the best people at the perfect time. I love when we're all together, just the feeling of that alone is enough. My sister and I can't wait to go back this upcoming Christmas. We love our mom again.

My Mom's House

both pieces by Omar Williams, 13

The more truthful you are in a family, the more secure a child is going to feel.
PHOTO AND CAPTION BY EVE HILL

My Friend Sharifa

I have always had trouble trusting people until this year. Sharifa and I had always hated each other, but now we find that we are exactly alike! The way she walks in a room, full of joy and passion for life. You can always tell when she's in a good mood: her hair is combed up in a nice ponytail, eyes glistening from the reflection of the light. Her cute little nose ring, small but perfect. Her lips, full and completely gorgeous!

Even though she is not perfect, chicken-legged and all, she knows that impurities are what makes a person better. I love her cute little smile and the innocent pout she gives me whenever she feels I don't give her enough attention! She always knows how to keep me in line — of course sometimes she doesn't do it in the best way! (She yells at me.) But it makes me know that she cares and loves me too! I know that friends like this, me and her, will always be together forever.

Friendship, to me, is the most important type of relationship. It's made of love, trust. Sincerity and hope. Love for one another! Trust between people, to be able to tell each other the most personal things. Sincerity, to show forgiveness and blessings. And hope, to be together forever, through thick and thin, and hope that life will be pleasurable as long as they are together.

Gaëla Bigras, 14

My Friend Sharifa

My Friend Gaëla

She has a smile that belongs to an angel. Her eyes are greeting and friendly. She's as wise as a saint and always tells the truth. She makes me feel special in every way. Her style is modest and not exaggerated. She is not judgemental. Sure she has her ups and her downs. But what can I say, she's human. Probably one of the best earthlings you'll ever meet. Her generosity is unexplainable. She's loyal and dynamic although at times annoying. But that's her personality. I'll never try to change her because she has never tried to change me. She has always made me feel unique. She has never judged me, even if I was wrong.

She's a strong individual who deserves respect, and I'll give her that much for all that she has given me. I'll stick with her through thick and thin. Comfort her to the end. Her name is Gaëla and she's a great friend.

Sharifa Delpeche, 16

My Friend Gaëla

The difference between two wonderful sisters—life as happiness and life as sadness.

PHOTO AND CAPTION BY ANDREW WATTLEY

I Used To Be/Now I Am

I used to be a little girl,
Now I am a young lady;

I used to be scared,
Now I am sure;

I used to be lost,
Now I am found;

I used to be quiet,
Now I am loud;

I used to be loved,
Now I am loved.

Tia Potter, 15

I Used To Be/
Now I Am

Love

The thing that gives me pleasure is love.

I am at my best when I give love and receive love.

It could be the kind of love you feel for a friend, or the kind of love you feel for a relative. It could be the love I have for a pet or the love I feel for a man. But whatever kind of love it is, it has to be genuine. I accept no substitute for the true meaning of love.

And what is love? It is God.

So, basically, my belief in God is what makes me happy and gives me strength to carry on, even when the hardest of times come along. Love is what makes me live. It's what makes me smile. It's what brings me joy in every sense of the word.

I love to love.

Angela Newby, 18

Sometimes you don't receive as much as you give. PHOTO BY JEREMY DUCHARME

PHOTO BY JAESON LEMAY

And the Room Glows

She has brown hair with deep green-grey eyes that can see when something is wrong. They can also see a lie.

She appears to be able to see your soul and the souls of the people close to God. She normally has wrinkles from the stress of the family, but when she smiles they are non-existent and the room glows.

In a way she is like a statue, a symbol of authority and control. But also loving, and caring, and understanding.

And the Room Glows

Danny Thorburn, 15

Working Hands

Her hands are rough and calloused, attesting to hard work, to cold winters without the gloves she keeps on losing. Dry, fine white lines crisscross the back of her hands, her brown hands. Short hands, not square, not oval, certainly not delicate.

"How's your day?" the gentle hand asks, patting, stroking, catching on my skin, the fibres of my clothes. Hard yet soft, accustomed to carrying four bags of groceries, scrubbing the floors, bleaching her uniform, ironing, washing, drying . . . Those same hands where lively eyes peek through after a joke, that gesture angrily, emphasizing her words, punctuating, exaggerating.

Her hands are rough and calloused, attesting to hard work . . . but always strong and gentle, firm and loving, guiding, never faltering.

Working Hands

Junie Desil, 19

Photo by Jessica MacAran

Set Me Free

As tear by tear is rolling
down the contours of my face,
my knowledge still is growing
as a result of my mistakes.
I can handle what they give me,
I can wipe my tears to see,
and as I stand there hoping
that someone will set me free
I realize time and time again
that someone must be me.
Without my pride, without my strength
my life would be but none.
So when I'm looking for
calling for
my saviour, I'm the one.
And now when a tear is rolling
down the contours of my face,
I let it keep rolling
'cause I know it'll make me strong.

Eve Hill, 19

Set Me Free

I love being together. Just the feeling of that alone is enough.

PHOTO BY JAZMIN MANNING / CAPTION BY OMAR WILLIAMS

I'm Here

Yes, I did have problems with my parents.
Yes, I did have problems with my peers.
Yes, I did have problems with school.
Yes, I had problems with fitting in.
No, I did not have self-esteem.
No, I did not have self-confidence.
No, I did not have understanding.
No, I did not have helping hands.
No, I did not have patience.
NOW I have self-confidence.
NOW I have self-esteem.
NOW I have patience.
NOW since I have those three I have
No problems with my parents.
I have no problems with my peers.
I have no problems with my school.
And I guess I now fit in, but that's me.
And it's been a long, long _______ long path,
But I'm here!

I'm Here

Charles Wagge, 18

The End of the Road

As I walk down the long dark road, I look around only to see that I'm all alone. All alone in a world of nothing. A blinding white light far ahead of me waits. I know there's no turning back. I can feel the thick white fog surrounding me. Coming down and caressing my face. The fog sweet and soothing. Almost like death. If I walk forward, I will be taken to a world full of love and peace where no one can hurt anyone. If I go back I will find myself trapped. Trapped like a fly in a spider's web. In a world of pain and hate, where I can trust no one, not even myself. But right now I stand alone and confused. There's no one around, nowhere to go. No one to take my hand and guide me home. So I turn and walk slowly towards the beautiful white light that awaits, at the end of the road.

Amanda Stillemunkes, 17

The End
of the Road

Let's not lose hope!

PHOTO BY HEATHER WRIGHT

I'm using my clarity as a tool to help others.

PHOTO BY JEREMY DUCHARME / CAPTION BY SEMIRA WEISS

Contributors

Please note that for the most part, the ages indicated are the ages at which the contributors began to work on this book.

Jonah Aspler, 16, has the kind of curious mind that makes for successful photojournalism. Jonah, who is also a musician, says, "I'm glad there is something that's causing kids to think about making a better world. I'm glad to be a part of L.O.V.E."

Saima Baig, 17, is particularly concerned about violence against children and women. When a close friend was stabbed to death in her own home, in her own bed, Saima's heart was broken. "I believe that every child on this earth is brought down as an angel," Saima writes, urging society to better protect its children from harm.

Judy Baser, 17, a new L.O.V.E. outreach leader, is on her way to a career as a professional photographer. Her exciting work earned her entry into Dawson College's highly acclaimed photography program. We are very proud of her.

Ian Berard, 18, looks back and writes, "I've hurt others and I've hurt myself" and ". . . it took the system three years to teach me to change my anger." Now Ian, a talented writer, uses his own painful experiences with violence to teach other youths to find alternate solutions to their problems.

Gaela Bigras, 14, joined L.O.V.E. in January 1998, even though it meant travelling by bus and metro for long hours through rain, snow, and sleet, *after* a full day at school.

Sherri-Lynn Burgess, 18, has been a committed L.O.V.E. member. She is determined to help children who are survivors of child abuse, through her writing, photographs, and videos.

Melissa Colley, 16, was in the first L.O.V.E. photojournalism group in January 1994. She is now the host of a Montreal-based television program, and a star member of the L.O.V.E. outreach teams, bringing the non-violence message into schools, boardrooms, and government offices.

Miranda Collins, 16, is a gifted writer. She has produced many excellent pieces of work since she joined L.O.V.E., travelling two hours, twice a week, to attend our photojournalism program. Her commitment is outstanding.

Tabitha Cross, 17, came to the photojournalism program with strong ideas and opinions about the issue of youth violence. She has contributed much to our learning.

Gabriel Cukier, 15, expresses anger and frustration effectively in his work. Gabriel joined L.O.V.E. in 1998, and will soon take an active role as a youth leader.

Teria Delaportas, 18, writes passionately about interpersonal relationships. Her piece "The Jacket" describes how "my love, my best friend, my world" was stabbed sixteen times, his life taken because someone wanted to steal his jacket. Teria says she'll do anything to stop the violence.

Sharifa Delpeche, 16, tries to fit some L.O.V.E. activities into a busy schedule of work and school. She doesn't always succeed, but she is a sensitive and evocative writer who uses her skill to explore her past and the universal need for love and understanding.

Meghann Delves, 18, is a world traveller. Her poetic writing takes us deep into the heart of a struggling young woman.

Junie Desil, 16, is one of the original L.O.V.E. kids and a former member of the board of directors. She is our first youth member to make it to university. We know many will follow. Junie is studying social sciences and plans a career working with kids. In this book, she addresses racial and parenting issues, using her clear and powerful writing style.

Some L.O.V.E. Kids

Jeremy Ducharme was 18 years old when he joined the photojournalism project, immediately exhibiting gifts in both writing and photography. Jeremy's picture of his own shadow photographing wildly aggressive graffiti captures the fury and torment which can erupt when anguish is not acknowledged and dealt with.

Ryan Dwyer, 18, has been able to use his experiences to educate and enlighten others. He has begun to see the power an individual has to make change.

Naomi Dylan, 14, is always enthusiastic and excited to join in on new L.O.V.E. programs. Her personal writings have touched many of us and have contributed to our outreach workshops. She is looking forward to beginning our outreach program this year.

Justin Fullerton, 14, came to Leave Out ViolencE to warn our readers that, even though many people may not want to know about it, the public must face the fact that gang violence, drugs, and other ugly activities are going on in Canadian cities. He writes with clarity and power.

Eve Hill, at 17, became L.O.V.E.'s first youth member. She also sat on the board of directors. Eve's main concern is the safety of children, how to better parent them, how to protect them. In a deceptively simple line, she writes "violence in entertainment becomes violence in our environment." It is a warning.

Jennefer Jenei, 16, brings unusual sensitivity and awareness to L.O.V.E. Her photo of a girl looking into a fountain makes us reflect on the courage it takes to face what so many young people have to deal with each day.

Krista Lajeunesse, 15, has taken a photo of two boys playing in the park which is calm and positive, presenting what life should be like for teens. However in the context of our themes, it suggests the sadness that can lie beneath the surface.

Patrick LaPointe's poem "I Can't Wait for It to Shine" describes the emotional rollercoaster on which so many youths live today. Patrick was 17 when he attended the photojournalism project.

Jaeson Lemay, 15, channelled some of his enormous energy into expressing interesting and challenging ideas about youth violence, and the poverty and drugs which underlie so much of it.

Anna Maria Lof, 17, joined L.O.V.E. to tell others that they had better do something about the rising tide of youth violence, especially violence committed by young girls and women. "Make a difference, make the future. Make it possible for our children to grow up in a safe environment," Anna Maria writes.

Jessica MacAran proved to be a natural writer at the age of 15. The tragic loss of a dear friend, who suffered years of abuse at home and then killed herself with a heroin overdose, brought Jessica to L.O.V.E. She now makes a tremendous contribution, warning other kids about drug use and emphasizing the critical need for victims of abuse to seek help.

Kate Martin, 19, is not only a strong leader and role model, she is also an excellent ambassador for non-violence in the community. Kate has spoken to children, youth, and adults in schools, conferences, and at many other community presentations.

Phillippe Martins, 16, uses the photojournalism project to warn others about the youth gangs and violence going on in the seemingly safe suburbs of Montreal, to show that society doesn't offer some kids many options, and to express what it feels like to be victimized.

Ali Mosadeq, 14, has grown into a strong L.O.V.E. member. He began coming to meetings with his brother simply as an observer. As soon as he was old enough, he started participating in the programs, and has contributed wonderful pieces of work.

Mohammed Mosadeq, 15, is involved in all aspects of the L.O.V.E. organization. He is a brilliant writer who continously challenges us to look critically at the world we live in, in order to work for change. Mo is actively involved in helping expand our programs to reach new goals.

Diederik Muylwyk, 16, has contributed to L.O.V.E. as a participant and a volunteer. He not only produces his own enlightening work, but helps others in the Toronto photojournalism program. His insights and ability to engage a group have added so much to our outreach program.

Malcolm Nadeau, 17, brought a wealth of sensitivity and experience to the photojournalism project. With courage, he recalled painful moments both as a way of coming to terms with his own past, and to show others that they are not alone in their struggles. Malcolm's voice effectively expresses the anguish of children and youths who are not heard.

Angela Newby, 18, found photojournalism an interesting and challenging experience. In her own quiet way she listened and shared opinions, and created wonderful pieces of work.

Teniesha Ochrym, 15, has been a Toronto L.O.V.E. member since it's inception. She is a dynamic speaker, and loves sharing her experiences with other children in order to help them.

Julia Paul, 17, confronted many youth issues when she joined L.O.V.E. Her poetic writing and strong photographs remain outstanding examples of what the project set out to do: capture youth culture — no holds barred. Julia is now an exceptional L.O.V.E. leader with a promising future.

Tiffany Payette, 15, has been a regular photojournalism participant in Montreal. Her outstanding photo, of a girl whose long hair drapes down to form a shelter over a friend she is comforting, reminds us of the enveloping power of love.

Tia Potter, 15, looks forward to working with the L.O.V.E. leaders to help them to bring the message of non-violence into the community. With her strong personality and original ideas she is bound to make a difference.

Anne Marie Raffoul is a member of the L.O.V.E. outreach program. She has always provided us with wonderful insights into the lives of young people. She is a very sensitive young woman.

Nicholas Ramirez, 17, joined L.O.V.E. and instantly began to make magic with a camera. His sensitive eye draws him to take photographs that touch our hearts.

Robert Robbins, 18, is a strong leader in the L.O.V.E. organization. He is a youth member on the Toronto Board of Directors and is a strong outreach participant. We are all excited to see Rob's leadership grow and expand in all areas of L.O.V.E.

Roxanne Ryder's photograph and caption about drug use always provokes controversy when we take it into classrooms to analyse the connection between drugs and violence. Roxanne, 17, writes, "They don't realize the down side to their Saturday night."

Natisha Ryner, 17, is a new member of L.O.V.E. She is involved in many community programs that promote non-violence, and provide youth with the opportunity to speak out. She is a valued asset to our organization and her community.

Melissa Samuel, 15, is a natural writer, producing, with seeming ease and certainly with grace, pieces about youth violence, abuse, and the immigrant experience. Her piece about gunshots in the school yard leaves the reader breathless.

Leana Satim, at 16, wrote a remarkable story about "A Boy I Know," whose family trauma led him to violence in a street gang. Her story raises an important issue: ". . . if maybe he had had someone to talk to from the start, some, or all of this might never have happened." This is the most important theme of *L.O.V.E. Works!*

Emmie Sheaf, 16, brought her dynamic personality to the photojournalism project along with a wealth of experience. She used both of these qualities to stimulate interesting discussions on the causes of and solutions to youth violence.

Jesse Sicinski, at 14, startled his editors with words and photos which took us into painful places, troubling fears. He expresses emotions with unflinching honesty. Jesse's courageous writing contributes to the success of this book as a wakeup call to the community.

Sabrina Smith, 17, effectively describes such human phenomena as the contrast between what *seems* to be and what actually *is*. She also writes about the baffling fascination with fighting she found among the students in her school, and how sad it is that so many girls resort to violence on the least provocation.

Amanda Stillemunkes, 17, has contributed immeasurably to L.O.V.E. through her creativity. Her writing has touched us all and her photographs always elicit discussion in our outreach presentations. We hope she continues to share this wonderful gift.

Sarah Topey, 17, has contributed enormously to the photojournalism project. Her insights are wise, her use of language is precise, and her experience with peer mediation is a great asset.

Danny Thorburn's description of how he felt during and after a fist fight is painfully evocative, and is an amazing contrast to his moving description of a person who loves and cares for him. These are two exceptionally sensitive pieces, written when he was 15.

Peggy Trougakos, 17, is interested in fighting violence both against adolescents and by them. She writes powerfully on these subjects, and will be an effective youth outreach leader.

Tess Vo's love of photography is a welcome addition to our photojournalism program. She shares her expertise with other L.O.V.E. members, lending them a hand whenever she can. Tess is 18.

Charles Wagge, 17, is a thoughtful, articulate youth leader. Originally from Alberta, Charles writes, "I have seen and heard pretty much all that a person of 17 can experience in the field of violence." He now lives in Montreal where he goes to school, works with L.O.V.E., and plans to make a career of improving the lives of others.

Andrew Wattley, 14, is involved in many L.O.V.E. programs, including photography, drama, outreach and video. His enthusiasm is always appreciated and he is constantly learning and growing.

Semira Weiss, 17, feels strongly about protecting the environment from the violence it sustains daily. Semira writes about the experiences she herself has had with violence, glad that they are all behind her. She writes, "I'm using my clarity as a tool to help others and help myself."

Omar Williams's photograph of a little girl doing her homework while the sun streams in across her page immediately became one of Leave Out ViolencE's most popular symbols of hope. Omar took this beautiful photograph when he was only 13 years old. He magically slipped into L.O.V.E. despite our requisite entry-level age of 14.

Colleen Wilson, 16, came to L.O.V.E. as a remarkable individualist in the middle of dealing with her own issues. She provided us with a powerful collection of poems and photos describing some of the most challenging aspects of youth culture today: drugs, sexuality, family life, Aids, and being called "different."

Matthew Woolcock, 16, wrote poetry for L.O.V.E. The photograph he produced for this book captures the joy achieved when you're engaged in something creative and challenging that you love to do.

When **Heather Wright**, 15, began with L.O.V.E., it was her passionate, sometimes angry writing which first attracted attention. But as an outstanding youth leader, she learned how to articulate her ideas so well aloud, that a senior business executive who heard her speak remarked, "I would vote for that young woman to be prime minister of Canada."

How to L.O.V.E.

How to Leave Out ViolencE

What We Want You to Know

If you are involved in violence, **you can get out**. Many of us have.

We have told you our stories so that you can see that **you are not alone**.

Keeping problems inside is not your only choice. **Tell somebody**. And if they don't listen, tell somebody else. And somebody else. Until somebody hears you. If you are persistent, somebody will. Just having your feelings acknowledged can break the tension that can lead to violence.

Many kids who have been touched by violence **take active steps** to stop it. You can too; trying to make a difference feels great!

Any child or youth in Canada can **get advice and/or help by calling the Kids' Help Line at 1-800-668-6868. Or, in the United States, call 1-800-422-4453.** You don't have to give your name unless you want to.

Dealing with the Feelings that Can Trigger Violence

If you feel that you are not good enough, **find even one positive person who accepts you the way you are**. Then let that person act as a mirror, reflecting back a positive image of yourself to you. Do the same for them.

Give yourself credit for your personal qualities and day-to-day accomplishments no matter how small they might seem.

People rarely disrespect others who respect themselves. You can **give yourself the respect you deserve**. It's a great place to start.

Avoid boredom. Be creative. Draw. Write. Make music. Dance. Sing. Play sports. Find a way to express yourself.

When you feel guilty about something, introduce yourself to your best self: **Do something kind for another person**.

Be your own guide. Think of where you want to be ten years from now and don't let others pressure you into doing things you feel uncomfortable with.

Remember that you are the only person who can control what you think. You can **replace negative thoughts with positive ones**. You have the power to change your thoughts.

When you are down on yourself, remember that life is so complex that no one can live without making mistakes. **Forgive yourself and move forward**.

Often, we can be depressed by a feeling that our lives are meaningless. A great way to overcome this is to **always have goals**. Have short-term goals like learning to sing or to run fast, and long-term goals such as trying to improve the environment. Try not to let yourself get distracted from pursuing your goals. The painful feeling of wanting things that others have can be reduced if you are busy achieving a positive goal like helping others or being creative.

Be aware that watching violence can make you more aggressive and fearful: **Limit your exposure to violent movies and TV**.

If you are being hurt by someone, whether physically, sexually, or emotionally, **talk to someone you respect.** Tell them what is happening to you. **Ask for help**.

Loneliness can lead to feelings of despair; **be part of a positive community** working to make a difference.

Why not **join Leave Out ViolencE**? Get involved! Call us in Montreal at 514-875-LOVE, or in Toronto at 416-483-6265. No matter where you live, we'll help you start a L.O.V.E. branch in your area.

Dealing with Anger

Remember that anger is a natural emotion.

You have the right to feel angry when you are hurt, exploited, ignored, manipulated, frustrated, cheated, or rejected. **But anger does not have to lead to violence**. You can choose to deal with your anger constructively.

Here's how:

Acknowledge that you are angry.

As soon as you possibly can, **tell the person(s) you are angry at why you are angry**. If that is not possible, at least speak to someone.

Sometimes anger is so extreme that we feel out of control. **Be aware of some normal physical signs of anger**, such as jitters, a flushed face, a racing heart, irregular breathing, stammering, and clenched fists.

You may need to take certain steps before you are ready to express your anger without violence. Some ideas are: **go for a walk, listen to your favourite song, punch a pillow, scream (but not at somebody), breathe deeply, count to ten**. As soon as you are able, go back and talk about why you are angry.

Express your anger clearly, and ask for a change in behaviour. Here are examples of how you could approach someone who has made you angry:

1) Say, "I am angry because you called me stupid. I deserve to be treated with respect."
2) Say, "I am angry because you ignore me when I am talking to you. I would appreciate your stopping to listen to what I have to say."

Some Ways the Community Can Help Prevent Youth Violence

Create after-school programs and get involved in running them.

Create programs for the whole community (such as picnics, sports events, social clubs) and get youth involved in the planning.

Make local businesses aware of what the community needs: flexible work hours for single and/or working parents, resources, opportunities for youth to work, etc.

Get involved with your child's school.

Arrange community forums that discuss problems or issues in the community, and invite youth to participate.

Plan multicultural events such as holiday and food festivals through community centres or schools.

Arrange for workshops in schools on such things as conflict or anger management, assertiveness training, and violence prevention.

Monitor media violence. Studies show that there is a significant correlation between viewing violence on TV and in movies and aggressive behaviour of the viewer. You can:

- Be aware of what your children watch and what video games they play. Discuss them.
- Tell them that language can be violent too.
- Offer your children alternatives to violent movies and TV. They can and will enjoy a range of films or programs that don't involve shoot-outs, car chases, serial killers, or armed bank robbers.

Some Discussion Questions for Educators, Parents, and Youth Leaders

Here are some examples of how the photographs in this book can be used to provoke discussion on issues related to violence, its causes, and its prevention.

Page 12 — Boy with children

- What type of person do you want to be in 10 years?
- Who are your heroes? Write them all down — people you know, people from TV, etc.
- What qualities do they have that make them your heroes?
- How can you be a good influence on younger kids?

Page 20 — Empty swings

- Where should children turn if they are being hurt physically, sexually, or emotionally?
- What can the community do to make outdoor play more safe?
- What is important for you to know about safety when you are outside your own home?

Page 28 — Graffiti

- What are some negative thoughts that kids can have?
- What does it feel like when people don't listen to you?
- When you listen to a friend, how does it make them feel?
- What positive actions can you take when you feel you are being ignored?
- Who can you talk to when your thoughts feel out of control?

Page 33 — Little girl

- What can you do if a friend, family member, or someone else in your life tells you that you are no good?
- How does a parent's feelings of self-esteem affect a child?
- How does the way you feel about yourself affect your behaviour?

Page 38 — Marijuana plant

- What are the effects of regular drug use?
- How do you deal effectively with peer pressure?
- What is the connection between drugs and violence?

Page 53 — The gun

- What does power mean to you?
- Suppose a person does use violence to get revenge. What happens next? And then what . . .? Where and how does it end?
- What are other options to "You hit me, so I'll give you a taste of your own medicine"?
- What do you think about all the violence on TV, in movies, in music, and in video games?

Page 64 — The rave

- Do you judge people because of how they look? If so, why?
- How does it make you feel if people judge you because of how you look, or because you are a young person?
- Give an example of how judging someone by how they look can lead to violence.

Page 80 — Four teens

- How does your community support its kids?
- What kind of after-school or weekend programs does your community offer?
- What kinds of support and programs would you like to see in your community?
- What can you do to help create a better community?

Page 90 — The staircase

- Why would someone want to end his life?
- What can you do if you feel sad, depressed, or helpless?
- If a friend confides that she has thoughts of suicide, what can you do?

Page 142 — Mother and child

- Describe a family that has poor communication.
- What are the consequences?
- Describe a family that has good communication.
- What are the consequences?